Carol Perera Weingeist

Best Wishes

Scarsdale Friends Meeting

P9-ARK-152

Made & printed in Great Britain.

APPROACH TO QUAKERISM

APPROACH TO QUAKERISM

E. B. CASTLE

*Professor of Education
in the University of Hull*

BANNISDALE PRESS · LONDON

Printed in Great Britain
by John Bellows Ltd, Gloucester

CONTENTS

M

IN MEMORIAM

Lord make me an instrument of Thy Peace.
 Where there is hatred, let me sow love;
where there is injury, pardon;
 where there is doubt, faith;
where there is despair, hope;
 where there is darkness, light;
where there is sadness, joy.
O Divine Master, grant that I may not
so much seek to be consoled, as to console;
 to be understood, as to understand;
to be loved, as to love.
 For it is in giving, that we receive;
it is in pardoning, that we are pardoned;
 it is in dying that we are born to
  eternal life.

ST FRANCIS OF ASSISI

INTRODUCTION

IN THE 1907 edition of *Quaker Strongholds* first published in 1890, Caroline Stephen tells us that 'It is now thirty-five years since I found in Friends' Meeting for worship what I must call the native element of my own inner life.' It is nearly thirty-five years since I made the same discovery and found a permanent home in the Society of Friends, an experience that has proved satisfying, consolidating and sometimes even exciting. This little book then, is written in a mood of gratitude and in the form of a broad statement of Quaker teaching that may help other seekers towards a faith that has given much satisfaction to me.

I write not as one who has arrived but as one who hopes he is on the way. A good deal of what I shall say is as much the product of doubt and failure as of conviction. This is so obviously the story of most seekers after certainty that I am comforted by the reflection that my experience is a common experience, and, maybe, will help some in the wide companionship of faithful doubters to realize that they have achieved more faith than they thought. For if there is one message more than another I wish to leave with those who attempt these pages it is that, in the end, to build bravely on the little conviction we have is the only means of entry into the realm of personal experience which at last enables us to say with Job — 'I know.'

I came to Quakerism through books; not perhaps the best way. I was at once attracted by its originality and freshness, by a kind of naïve perception of fundamentals that enabled the early Friends, so often untutored people, to get behind forms to the truths that forms obscured. There seemed to be in these seventeenth-century pioneers a capacity to direct religion into every corner of life, into the intimately personal but also into the social and political life of their time. Religion was not for them a verbal confession but a dynamic experience that impelled them to re-examine human behaviour, to re-interpret the Scriptures and to give a new and an intensely practical turn to Christian belief. As I studied the progress of Quakerism through the last three

9

centuries it appeared to possess a self-adjusting modernity that preserved its relevance to new knowledge and to changes in the human situation. Its appeal seems specially directed to those who hesitate to formulate belief but desire, nevertheless, to commit themselves to a Christian way of life.

Gradually, as I read on, and began to attend a Friends' Meeting for Worship, the odd pieces in my religious jig-saw puzzle began to slip into place. I began to see that some Christian orthodoxies which I had not been able to accept became, on Quaker interpretation, at least more acceptable. What particularly appealed to me at that time was the direct way in which the Quaker insistence on the quiet inward life became inevitably associated with its active outward expression in the world of affairs. In Quakerism I found the Christian and the social to be effortlessly intertwined.

One of the obstacles to religious commitment that besets so many people who seek companionship within a religious community is their sense of unworthiness. This is a wholly healthy sign of a proper pride that springs from an honest mind. 'I am not good enough to be called a Christian,' you declare. Of course you aren't; few men are, if by Christian you mean a Christian saint, who has achieved a likeness to Christ as near as is possible for a man born of woman. 'I am not good enough to apply for membership of the Society of Friends.' Of course you aren't. There are few members of the Society called Quakers who are worthy of membership of the community to which they belong, if by membership we imply that they are as good as they ought to be or even as good as they try to be. The Church, Jesus said, is for sinners only.

What is implied by 'Christian' and 'membership' in this connection is rather that our faces should be turned towards Christ, that we admit His leadership even if we fail as His disciples. Jesus knew that the builders of His Kingdom would be unworthy folk. There were not in His day, and there are not today, enough men and women of any other kind. Similarly, to become a member of the Society of Friends is not an assumption of worthiness but the avowal of a hope that the beliefs and methods of the Quaker way of life are for some of us the best way of worshipping, believing and working in Christ's name.

Experience within the Society, with Quakers as distinct from

Quakerism, was both a disillusionment and an increasing fulfilment. I soon learned that Quakers were not the same as Quakerism;
any more than Christians are the same as Christianity. My
disillusionment was the foolishness of a book-convinced novice;
what mattered, I eventually realized, was that I found myself
amidst a group of ordinary people, a high proportion of whom
in unobtrusive or more evident ways, were really concerned to
put a sorry world to rights, and that the spur to their endeavour
was a Christian faith growing out of individual experience.

This book is not, then, another history of the Society of Friends,
but rather an attempt to present Quakerism as an interpretation
of Christian teaching relevant to the condition of our world
today. The approach is quite personal; and, as it came about that
my entry into the Quaker fold was by way of the historical path,
several chapters record this earlier appeal to my thinking. The
order of the chapters does in fact reflect my personal approach.
First come the *Foundations* upon which Quakerism grew; then the
Implications or extensions of basic Quaker beliefs that seem
inevitably to follow from these foundations; and finally the
Applications of Quaker faith to the great social world in which
all men and women live. I trust that in this way I have been able
to present a record of the growth of Quakerism without too
much historical reference and a picture of the nature of Quaker
belief and practice that is more than a religious tract.

As this is not a work of scholarship but a book for the general
reader, I have thought it better not to confuse the text with
references and footnotes. I hope that the brief bibliography at the
end of the book and the acknowledgments made in the text, will
be sufficient recognition of my debt to those whose words I have
quoted. I must add that some of the phrasing in the last three
chapters is similar to that in relevant parts of my two small books
The Undivided Mind and *Building the New Age*, both now out
of print.   E.B.C.

Hull, Christmas 1960.

PART I

Foundations

I

THE BEGINNINGS

'Many sons have done virtuously in this day, but dear George thou excellest them all.'

WILLIAM PENN

I HAVE referred in the Introduction to the 'originality' of Quakerism. This may be misleading; for it would be quite wrong to assume that the first generation of Quakers claimed to have discovered something new. On the contrary, they were convinced that they were reviving something very old — the primitive Christianity of apostolic times, whose sweetness and power, they believed, had been overlaid for centuries by the controversies, theologies, rituals and massive organization of the historic church. Nor were the testimonies and beliefs we associate with the Society of Friends peculiar to the followers of George Fox, the founder of the Society. For there were in the seventeenth century, and especially during the years 1640–60, a vast company of laymen ardently seeking a more intimate and personal expression of faith than the Anglican and Calvinistic churches offered them. This body of 'seekers' had emerged out of the religious ferment that had both preceded and followed the Protestant revolution throughout Western Europe, and in England had produced that special brand of revolutionary religion we call Puritanism.

Commonwealth England was swarming with small groups of pious enthusiasts who were casting aside age-long practices and experimenting with new forms of worship. These 'seekers' constituted the most radical wing of Puritanism and eventually suffered the bitterest persecution from the conservative wing of the reforming churches. Several characteristics they had in common: in their meetings they dispensed with the mediating function of the priest; they resisted and rejected the ancient authority of the church and its hierarchy; with much daring they began to interpret the Scriptures in new ways. One other characteristic common to the 'seekers' was to be of great importance

15

to the growth of Quakerism: they were inheritors, often crude and mistaken in the interpretation of their inheritance, of that long-mystical tradition fed by the Hebrew prophets and the Christian saints. This, the most personal, the most intense and yet the most elusive and inexplicable part of the religious life, was to become the central religious reality for early Friends. It is possible that this mystical emphasis, so characteristic of this period of expectancy, was partly stimulated by the influence of continental mystics, whose writings had appeared in England in the middle of the century, but there seems to be no weighty evidence that this was so. In any case such a stimulus was hardly needed, for the spiritual stirring and radical thinking that marked the religious climate of that age was sufficient to ensure that these mystical trends would be a native growth.

There has been no period in English history when ordinary men and women thought more intelligently about personal religion, or when the roots of faith and the relevance of the Scriptures to the intimate affairs of daily life were more radically examined, than in the seventeenth century. This was pre-eminently the century when what he believed about God and God's word mattered most to the common man. There were thousands of men and women in England who felt constrained to reject the mediation of priest and ordained minister and seek a faith founded on personal experience. These scattered and unorganized groups of 'seekers' who had forsaken established religious practices were the seed-bed of Quakerism. And it was into this turmoil of expectancy that in 1643 the young George Fox, laying down his shoe-maker's awl, turned his back on the church in which he was born to seek release from the burden of his perplexities.

Quakerism, then, was in the making before George Fox gave it form and direction. It may not be necessary to begin our studies of Quakerism with the work of Fox, but we shall soon have to turn to him if we wish to discover where the essence of Quakerism lies, for it was from his ardent seeking and travail that the original essence of Quakerism was distilled. There were many others working with him who shall be named where necessary, but he is the dynamic figure and the leader among the first generation of Friends, the rightly adjudged founder of the Society. He was truly an original and 'no man's copy'. I found in him an irresistible attraction, partly because of his amazing personality — clear as a bell, hard as granite, yet tender as a child, sensitive always to the vision and calls of another world which was as real to him as the rough paths on which he trod in his incessant journeyings — and also because we find in this rude prophet, the Amos of protestant rebellion, a man who can bridge for us with penetrating perception and yet in homely terms,, the chasm that so often divides the world of sense from the elusive world of spiritual reality. Fox's spiritual struggle is presented to us in a form which enables us to believe that even less gifted men and women can at least catch a glimmer of an experience that was vivid and real to him.

This remarkable, untutored man seemed constantly to be exposing simple but fundamental and *workable* truths that lay behind verbal obscurity and symbol and written declarations of faith. As his cultured friend and follower William Penn said of him, 'he much laboured to open Truth to the people's under-standings and to bottom them upon the principle, and principal, Christ Jesus'. It was this constant 'bottoming' that was striking ; his gift of breaking through the crust of seeming to the essence lying hidden beneath appearances. He 'would go to the marrow of things' says Penn. Abrupt, disjointed as his utterances often were, they always seemed to crystallize into 'sensible practical truths, tending to conversion and regeneration and the setting up of the Kingdom of God in the hearts of men'.

Lest my admiration for George Fox tempts me to pass the bounds of truth, let me quote from a source unlikely to commit this error — from Ronald Knox's *Enthusiasm:*

'His stature is somewhat heroic. Allow, if you will, for a certain amount of exaggeration when he tells you, in the *Journal,* how instantaneous were the effects of his preaching, how easily he puts his adversaries to silence; discount the egotism, if you can call it egotism, of a man wholly absorbed in his mission. Remember only that this is a man, full of scruples and questionings in his youth, who without (it seems) any agonies of conversion has emerged into a state of complete spiritual equilibrium, is sure of himself in all companies and upon all occasions. Watch him walking barefoot through the streets of a cathedral town, ingeminating "Woe to the bloody city of Lichfield", interrupting the sermons of the ministers in their steeple houses, and preaching at them from the floor of the church, allowing street-boys to pelt him and roll him in the mud, lecturing the magistrates when he appears before them, refusing to eat with the Lord Protector after his interview. Call him Don Quixote if you like, but remember St Ignatius. . . . And his companions how they multiply, how they develop into lesser replicas of himself! They go everywhere; they try to convert the Pope, they try to convert the Sultan.'

As a person not specially gifted with the mystical apprehension which Fox and many early Friends possessed, I found increasing appeal in a type of mysticism in which the subject never remained in rapt and self-satisfying contemplation of an infinite Beyond, but always swung back from the mystic vision into the world which ordinary men called 'real'. There was a strong savour of practicality in Fox's mysticism, a robust commonsense, that appeals to normal sentient men, reminding them that the mystic vision can be relevant to the day's work. What Fox was and what he experienced of divine revelation and grace he always presented as possible for all.

Penn has written that George Fox was 'a discerner of other men's spirits and very much a master of his own'. This discernment was observable in his innumerable contacts and contests with all conditions of men, from the Protector Cromwell to the tavern brawlers and jailors who punctuated his rough passages among the common folk of England. In a true sense this was the rare gift of imagination. It was not poetic or literary imagination but the imagination that enables us to get inside other people's minds, to feel with them, even to breathe with them. It was this imaginative sympathy with another man's condition that could evoke tears from the stern Protector's eyes and penetrate through the coarse obtuseness of bullying persecutors. But the amazing converting power which Fox seemed to exercise over even the least promising of wicked men, cannot be wholly attributed to his blessed gift of imagination, almost boundless as it was. His discernment of the spirits of men was also a product of his view of the nature of man. What Fox and early Friends had done was, to use Rufus Jones's phrase, 'to pass over to a new centre'; not, as the Protestant reformers had done, from the Church as centre to the Bible as centre, but further still — from the Bible as centre to the spiritual nature of man as the starting point of changing men's lives.

It was this shocking and dangerous heterodoxy that firmly compelled my attention. I studied the theme in Robert Barclay's *Apology* and in John William Graham's *The Faith of a Quaker* and in Fox's own words and experience, and saw opening out a new world of revelation and applications. Here was a demand, an entirely Christian demand it seemed to me, that required a man not to accept a faith on any other authority but the experience of Christian truth as he progressively worked it out in his own mind and soul.

What was this new method of attaining certainty which was focused for me in the lives and teaching of early Friends?

I KNEW EXPERIMENTALLY

There is one, even Christ Jesus, that can speak to thy condition.'
GEORGE FOX

FOX WAS not only a preacher of great power but the compiler of a journal that records his 'openings' of spirit and encounters with men and women throughout his unceasing travels in England and the eastern provinces of America. He was also a furious controversialist. He produced more than two hundred tracts and wrote hundreds of *Epistles* to the encouragement and guidance of his friends. It is from these records that we gain our knowledge of the principles that informed his teaching. All these writings are marked by a clear inward conviction, often obscurely expressed, which nevertheless consistently related the truth he discovered in moments of enlightenment with the lives of ordinary men.

Fox's years of spiritual perplexity, which began in early youth, his tussles with priests and 'professors' of established creeds who offered him no inward satisfaction and release, culminated in his Damascus vision. Early in his *Journal* he records under the year 1647:

'But as I had forsaken all the priests, so I left the separate preachers also, and those called the most experienced people; for I saw there was none among them that could speak to my condition. And when all my hopes in them and in all men were gone, so that I had nothing outwardly to help me, nor could I tell what to do, then, oh then, I heard a voice which said, "There is one, even Christ Jesus, that can speak to thy condition," and when I heard it my heart did leap for joy. . . . And this I knew experimentally.'

Now without that last sentence of this most quoted of Fox's utterances, his discovery might seem unremarkable. Did not all

Christians, including Fox's persecutors, believe that Christ was their saviour? The essence of Fox's experience lay in all that follows from his declaration that he knew *experimentally*. This emphasis on personal experience is the core of Quakerism. Fox believed that he had found the Real Presence, a spirit within himself, that ruled above all ecclesiastical regulation or man-made liturgy or clerical direction, or theologies and creeds. Far from being the product of unbounded presumption it was the outcome of a profound humility. The seeker in his wanderings had 'come home to within' and found, as Rufus Jones has said, 'the actual formation of the spirit of Christ in the fibre and structure of the inner life'. It was not a theory of salvation that Fox had worked out in the quiet of his study; not even a blessed sense of salvation in a flash of ecstatic conversion. It was the certainty that he had discovered the *source* of salvation, not in intellectual acceptance of a theological concept, but in the living Christ at work in his own soul. And more than this: that salvation from sin and despair depended on his obedience to the Christ spirit, on living through-out a life-time in harmony with it.

It seemed to me, as the implications of this revealing heresy slowly dawned upon me, that Fox had made personal and active and potently relevant to the condition of modern men, the ancient doctrine of the Holy Spirit. He had taken it out of its purely doctrinal trinitarian setting, rendering it warm and inti-mate, yet demanding and positive, in human persons. What was once remote, no more than one of the attractive metaphors of the Fourth Gospel, now became insistent and real, in me and around me in the present. In brief, something to be reckoned with.

The first impact on my mind of this new way of looking upon the relationship between men and Christ was a very simple one. I remembered that Jesus had declared that 'the Kingdom of God is within you'; that the prologue to St John's Gospel began with a statement regarding the spiritual nature of the universe, declar-ing that the Word was in the beginning, that the Word was God, that the Word became flesh, that the Word, 'the true light, even the light which lighteth every man' was coming into the world; that this Light was Christ. Finally, I remembered that a consistent theme of St Paul's life and teaching was summed up in his words: 'Christ within you is the hope of glory'; and again, 'I live; and yet no longer I, but Christ liveth in me'. This was but a beginning: George Fox's daring claim that every man had within him the Light of Christ seemed to derive some authority from Scripture. And yet it was not scriptural authority that gave Fox this 'opening', it was his own experience, as it was Paul's experience (for Paul had no New Testament), that Christ dwelt in some measure in the human soul if so be one might find Him.

Fox's *Epistles* teem with references to this Light or Seed. Here are a few examples among hundreds:

'Keep within . . . for the measure is within, and the Light of God is within, and the Pearl is within you, which is hid; and the Word of God is within you, and ye are the Temples of God, and God hath said, He will dwell in you and walk in you.'

'Stand still in the Light and submit to it. . . . And when Temptations and Troubles appear, sink down in that which is pure and all will be hush'd and fly away.'

'Mind the Light of God in your consciences . . . ; dwelling in it guides out of the many things into one Spirit.'

'Mind that which is pure in one another which joins you together; for nothing will join or make fit, but what is pure; nor unite, nor build, but what is pure.'

'Mind the pure Seed of God in you, and the mighty power of God will cherish you up to the Lord above all Temptations, not to bow down to anything.'

'Mind that Light in you that shows you Sin and Evil.'

'In the Light dwell that ye may come to know the Movings of the Spirit of Life in you.'

'Dwell in the Light . . . that to the Light, which is of God, people's minds may be directed and they come to receive the Life, and to witness it, that gave forth the Scriptures.'

'So the Seed know one in another, which Seed is Christ.'

Only the superficial reader will fail to see in these injunctions far more than the formless utterances of a man caught up in an inexpressible mystical experience. If we can for a moment catch some of the *concreteness* of this seemingly abstract terminology, we shall discover an amazingly vital and practical quality in Fox's words. It was, indeed, their relevance to human conduct and personal attitudes to other men that most concerned Fox. His advice to the thousands of scattered followers who read them have as solid a content as Paul's letters to his own struggling churches in the Mediterranean world. These phrases — 'the Light of God', 'the pure Seed', 'that which is pure'— referred to the inner core of personality, our deepest self, which, because of its divine origin and quality, was the spring of decision and action in every man. We are asked to *mind* the Light, to have it dominantly in mind, and obey it, submit to it and *use* it. And what will then happen? First, the Light will unite us in sympathy with other men; we shall be in 'one spirit' with them; we shall be 'joined' to them. Again, it will 'build' us up, integrate our personality into a harmonious working whole; enabling us to be 'above' temptations. Again, the Light will both reveal sin to us, in ourselves and in others, and at the same time keep us 'above' it. We are not asked to fear sin, to be over-conscious of the presence of evil, but to look within at the Light which reveals sin and in this Light to pass sin by. These applications of the doctrine of the indwelling Christ will receive fuller treatment later. They are mentioned here to indicate the intensely practical import of what at first glance seems to be obscure or meaningless.

If we require evidence of the impact of Fox's ministry on the conduct of this first generation of Quakers we have only to turn to the record of their sufferings. However muddled in their theology they may have been, we are constrained to sit loose to academic niceties when we see the quiet heroism with which they faced a hostile world. Heroism is never ridiculous even when displayed in a doubtful cause. In 1680 there were about 40,000 Friends in England. For a considerable number of years there were never less than 1,000 in jail, and it is estimated that between the years 1661 to 1697 nearly 14,000 Friends had suffered imprisonment, of whom 338 had died, either in prison or at the hands of their persecutors. Fox himself endured eight imprisonments, totalling six years. When men suffer and die for the truth as they see it, the cause is at least worthy of examination.

In early manhood Fox's 'opening' that 'there is one, even Christ Jesus, that can speak to thy condition', had not rid him of an overpowering sense of evil in the world, and this weighed as a great burden on his mind. He lays his perplexity before God:

'I cried to the Lord saying, "Why should I be thus seeing I was never addicted to commit these evils?" And the Lord answered that it was needful that I should have a sense of all conditions, how else should I speak to all conditions? And in this I saw the infinite love of God. I saw also that there was an ocean of darkness and death; but an infinite ocean of light and love which flowed over the ocean of darkness. In that I also saw the infinite love of God and I had great openings.'

In this second much quoted account of Fox's convincement we find the key both to his acceptance of suffering and to his power to ride above it. He saw God's love at work in the knowledge that he must recognize evil in evil men, suffer with them and at their hands, so that he might 'speak to their condition'; that is to say, respond to their need. Here God's wisdom and Fox's practical sense walked hand in hand. In facing evil he saw also the way to overcome it — not to run away from it but to immerse in the ocean of light and love that flows over and submerges the ocean of darkness. 'Stand in the Light', 'in the Light dwell'. he beseeches the struggling groups of Friends on both sides of the Atlantic.

This theme of Fox's to 'keep over' all tribulations recurs insistently in his writings. In his letters to perplexed men and women there are many versions of the theme, all concentrating on the practical efficacy of keeping *above* what tries you: 'be kept on top of the world' he says; 'look over all prisons'; 'keep over all bustlings', 'do not look at but keep over all unnaturalness; be 'above'; come 'over' that which is evil. And to his wife who was worried about the tenancy of her home, 'as to the house, keep over it'. When a Parliament man tells him he is to be sent to Smithfield to be burnt 'I told him I was over their fires and feared them not.' To Cromwell's daughter, Lady Claypole, he writes 'Do not look at the temptations, confusions, corruptions, but at the Light that discovers them, that makes them manifest; and with the same Light you will feel over them.'

Fox accepts the fact of human sin; there seems to be no evidence to suggest that he believed men to be born good. But he was much more concerned to lead men out of the futilities that beset the sinful life than to explain the existence of evil. Nor did Fox or Barclay say that the Light within a man's heart was the sole source of guidance, but rather that the Light within comes from without, a gift from God, the Source, to whom men must turn. To express this conception in theological terms is to say that God is both Immanent (near, within) and Transcendent (beyond). If then, we remain content with the idea that we only have to turn 'within' for guidance, we shall not be interpreting Quaker teaching correctly. We shall be confusing a part with the whole of Quaker belief. And by so doing we shall be moving away from the Christ-centred religion which Quakerism certainly is, to a debilitating confidence in the sufficiency of our own meagre measure of the Light. Furthermore, if we accept the Christ-centredness of Quakerism we must not only 'turn to within', although this is how we begin, but also to the outward Scriptures which reveal what Christ did and who He is. Quakerism then, does not preach the sufficiency of the Light within each erring soul, but rather the necessity for making our discovery of its power in ourselves the starting point of our excursion into the realms of truth and reality. This emphasis is made here because it is vital to begin with what we *know*, not with what we hope to know.

III

SHINING THROUGH ALL

*'Now the Lord God hath opened to me by His invisible power how
that every man was enlightened by the divine light of Christ; and I saw
it shine through all.'*

GEORGE FOX

WILLIAM PENN tells us that Friends usually spoke of 'the Light of
Christ within' rather than of 'the Light within'. This unhesitating
Christian emphasis is important, for it establishes firmly the fact
that the founders of Quakerism had no doubt whatever that their
faith was Christ-centred and Christ derived. This must be our
starting point, as Fox so emphatically declares in his letter to
Friends in Carolina in 1672:

> 'Dear Friends, to whom is my love in the blessed Seed,
> which . . . changeth not, which is the First and Last, in whom
> you have your Life and Peace with the God of Peace. So you
> few that are that ways keep your Meetings, and meet together
> in the name of Jesus, whose Name is above every Name . . .
> and you gathering in his Name where salvation is, he is your
> Prophet, your Shepherd, your Bishop, your Priest, in the
> midst of you, to open to you, and to sanctifie you, and to feed
> you with Life, and to quicken you with Life. Wait in his
> Power and Light, that ye may be Children of Light, by
> believing in the Light which is the Life in Christ, that you may
> be grafted into Him, the true Root, and built upon Him, the
> true Foundation who . . . is the Rock of Ages, yea of the Ages
> of the Prophets; of the Ages of His Apostles, and of the Ages
> of His People now. . . .'

This fervent letter, written in his maturity, can leave little doubt
concerning the Christ-centredness of Fox's teaching.

But what does Fox mean when he declares 'the Light which
is life in Christ' to be the sustaining power not only of the apostles

who knew Christ, not only of 'people now' but also of the prophets of Israel who did not know Christ? Here we are plunged into a controversy that bitterly separated Friends from the Puritan groups of their day. Fox is here declaring that the Light existed even before the advent of Jesus Christ, as a divine principle established in the very nature of man; that although we see in Christ this divine Light in full measure and in perfect expression, yet, in smaller measure, it shines dimly in all men, at all times and of all faiths, even in the wicked and the heathen. This was the central principle of Quakerism that distinguished it from all other Protestant belief. George Fox, William Penn and Robert Barclay, declared the Light to be universal; neither a special dispensation available only to men since Christ's advent, nor, as in the austere teaching of Calvin, a grace given to a small group of the 'elect'.

The Puritan sects amidst whom Quakerism was born, who also used the same terms — 'Light' and 'Seed' — but in a different sense, had, we must admit, a clearer view of the historical import of Christ's appearance on earth. Orthodox Christianity had always regarded this event as a watershed in human history, providing in the Incarnation, the Resurrection and the receiving of the Holy Spirit at Pentecost, a means of redemption for sinful man not available before Christ's advent. To the strict Calvinist, who believed that only the 'elect' could be saved, the wild assumption that the saving Light had been given to all men from the beginning of time, was a wicked blasphemy. To those who believed that there can be no salvation except through the offices of the Church — or, to quote William Penn's irreverent summary of the principle, 'out of a church, out of faith; not Dipt, not Christian'd' — this charitable conception of sinful man was equally shocking. It was this heresy that most embittered the disputes between Friends and Puritans in that disputatious age.

Two worlds faced one another: the world of tradition, of authoritarian theology, of logically formulated doctrine and Bible-based belief, and the world of inner individual spiritual experience; an experience that at the same time convinced Friends of the infinite grace of God and of the inborn capacity of ordinary men to respond to it. In Fox's reading of the Scriptures he saw the Light at work in the hearts of men in the Old Testament:

Penn, who had a scholar's knowledge of the ancient classical
world discerned in 'Socrates' good spirit' and in 'Plato's eternal,
ineffable and perfect principle of truth', evidence that the 'Eternal
Word' dwelt in man before Christ. He even places Pythagoras in
the picture. It cannot be said that Penn makes out a very good
case, but it is worth noting that some of the early Christian
Fathers, educated in a strongly classical background, were per-
turbed that so many noble spirits of the ancient world were born
too soon for salvation. It has been said of Penn that he wrote in
the spirit of Justin Martyr, of whom Rendel Harris has remarked
that 'when he saw Socrates struggling in the sea, he was not
content merely to throw him a rope to assist his salvation, but
he hauled him on board the ship of Christian faith, and bade him
make himself at home with the crew'. I mention these apologetics
of Penn to indicate the efforts that were made to justify a dogma,
for it is a dogma, that had not in the first instance been formulated
by argument or the study of texts, but communicated directly
by Fox's inward experience.

Quakerism also had in Robert Barclay a formidable apologist
of considerable theological scholarship. In his famous *Apology* he
asserts that 'God hath communicated and given unto every man
a measure of the Light of His own Son, a measure of grace, or a
measure of the Spirit' and that this gift has been made to every
man 'whether Jew or Gentile, Turk or Scythian, Indian or
Barbarian'. But Barclay does not rest here. He presents his critics
with two propositions: first, that 'those that have the Gospel and
Christ outwardly preached unto them, are not saved, but by the
working of the grace and light in their hearts'; and secondly, that
'many may be saved, to whom the gospel hath never been outwardly preached and who are utterly ignorant of the outward
history of Christ'.

In all these assertions of early Friends — that in all times and
even among the unbelievers, there lives this principle working
for righteousness — there was a tenderness and consideration for
those usually thought to be outside the barriers of salvation that
makes an immediate human appeal. And yet, after all, this was
but a charitable assumption — or at most a hypothesis on which
we can work. But for Fox it was much more than an assumption.
Like St Joan, Fox had his 'voices', a usual experience of the mystic,

and these voices had told him two things: first, that Christ could speak to his condition, and secondly, that there was in every man a capacity for response to divine leadings that Fox could only describe as the Christ spirit working as leaven within the human soul. What the theologians call Christology — the ideas about the nature of Christ and His relation to God and to man — was not very clearly worked out in Fox's thinking. His was an intuitive rather than a logical mind, and his knowledge of theology was of the most rudimentary kind. Indeed, Friends have never been completely successful in defining what the divine Light in man really is, because their conviction, after a point, defies definition.

But there was another form of witness at work, of very great importance, which bridges the gap between visionary revelation and its validity in the lives of men. In his encounters with all conditions of men, some of them marked by a rude brusqueness, others by a winning tenderness, Fox was certain that he saw the leaven working. He saw it in sudden changes of demeanour, in the blush of contrition, in swift shades of a new comprehension dawning in his enemy's eyes; in subtle changes of front that suggested no more than the acceptance of the possibility that there was some truth in what he said. Sometimes the response was positive and obvious, leading to joy and conviction and a changed life. Thus, Fox saw, with his own physical eyes, the evidences of the Seed stirring into life.

It was, then, Fox's experience that one only had to observe men's response to the promptings of their better selves to be certain that the Seed lay dormant but not dead in the hearts of his jailors and persecutors. Here he is observing no more than we can observe for ourselves if our discernment is sympathetically directed. But he drew a startling conclusion from his observation — that it was the indwelling Christ in evil men that was at work in them. This conviction clashed head-on with the Puritan view that only after conversion could a man be said to have the Christ spirit within him. For Fox, the Seed was planted in all men and its growth was a slow process fed by obedience to its prompting. Thus Fox staked his life's work on the conviction that he saw the Light 'shine through all'.

Perhaps a more striking and even more attractive evidence of the Light among the unconverted comes from the encounters with the Indians, recorded by Fox, Penn and John Woolman, and many American Friends in the American colonies. Fox, for example, records his experiences during a trek of two hundred miles in rough Indian country and notes the loving kindness of the Indians who helped the little group across rivers, and housed and fed them: 'And I came to an Indian King's house and he and his Queen received me and laid me on a mat for a bed, to lie by him, a very pretty man.' Many times he refers to the Indians as 'tender and loving' and receptive to his teaching. A Bristol Friend, Josiah Coale, who had visited America, writes that 'we found these Indians more sober and Christian-like toward us than the Christians so-called'. It was with such experiences in mind that Fox was prompted to reply to one of his bitter critics: 'the Light which doth enlighten every man that cometh into the world, by whom the world was made, was before natural conscience was, or natural light either. . . . And many of the Indians do show forth more in their conversations of the Light than you do'.

This is not proof that man's body is the temple of the Holy Spirit, but it is supporting evidence that early Friends were discovering for themselves a capacity in the hearts of men that would revolutionize their attitudes towards all mankind. It was a working hypothesis fraught with many practical consequences, as we shall see, and also a belief full of joyous and creative optimism. It pointed to a path that started from our own door and led hopefully but not smoothly to a solution of many vexing problems. Far from being an easy way to redemption from sin and despair it demanded strenuous exercise of all men's faculties in living a life of witness not only to the Light in ourselves but also to the Light in our neighbour.

To suggest that such an experience was unique to Friends would be to travesty truth. The whole contention of Fox and his followers was that this two-way traffic, not only between men of loving disposition, but between the loving and the unloving, had happened throughout history. Indeed, if early Friends had known as much of the medieval Christian saints as we could have wished, they would have found in the lives of these men and women, supremely in St Francis, attractive illustrations of their dominant conviction. It was the conclusion drawn from this evident capacity among 'people now' to act, even fitfully, in a Christ-like way, that became the special contribution of Friends to Christian views concerning the nature of human beings. It seemed to me that in an intuitive and illogical way early Friends had performed a kind of archaeological excavation and had stumbled on the missing links between God, Christ, the Scriptures and ourselves, finding these links beneath the accretions of man-made ritual and outward practices that had piled high upon the lower layer of gospel Christianity. To use again Penn's telling phrase, they seemed to have 'bottomed' the religious and human situation.

Finally, it must be noted, the capacity of men to act in a Christlike way does not mean that they will always think in the same way. When Fox, Penn and Barclay declared all men to be participants in the divine gift of the Inward Light they were making a general statement about the nature of men; they were not saying that each man's illumination would lead him to think like all other men similarly enlightened. The interpretation of our guidance remains an individual matter; the way we determine to become more like Christ lies with us; what we believe about the central tenets of the Christian faith, the nature of Christ and of God, must be a product of personal experience and seeking. What matters is that we be faithful to the Light we have. The Light will shine on our path; we decide where to tread. So great a freedom has its dangers, which have been evident in the Society of Friends from the earliest days, but they have been at least partially overcome by the gradual emergence of a community of fellowship loosely organized in a lay democracy which, while affording wide scope for a variety of belief, has preserved the essential Quaker emphasis.

IV

FROM UNBELIEF TO HERESY

'There was the light, the true light, which enlightened every man—coming into the world.'

JOHN. I. 9.

I HAVE SAID that one of the results of reading about George Fox and early Friends was to make intimate and real what had once been impersonal and remote. I was not worried about theology; I was concerned to find a faith that I could fit into, so to speak, being dimly aware of the danger of accepting a faith that fitted into me. To embrace a faith that fits us comfortably is a poor way of accepting religion; more than that, it is in a real sense a wrong and pernicious way, for it reverses the true order of things, placing the person who is to be re-formed into the position of the Truth that is to re-form him. It is an impiety that transposes creature and Creator. Faith must be a continuing challenge to which we must respond, a discipline to which we must submit, not a feather bed to protect us against the sharp edge of living. What I was seeking was a belief that, while commending itself to my reason, at the same time touched me as a person, a working faith which brought me even in microscopic measure into the realm of personal relationship which Jesus had with God.

From youth up I had always found it difficult to associate personality with the creator of the physical universe. The appalling vastness seemed to preclude a personality behind it. And how much more difficult it is today in our era of the expanding universe and space travel. Nevertheless, I had always been dimly conscious of another universe, a realm in which the spirit of man had soared high in spiritual and moral conquest. But where did a personal God fit into this spiritual world, what relationship existed between the physical and the spiritual realms? The ancient cry of Job is the cry of modern man: 'O that I might know where I might find him!'

It was in this connection that the first part of the jig-saw began to fit into place. The solution for me emerged as an application of the conception of the Inner Light to the doctrine of the Incarnation. Often had I wished that I could accept this doctrine as presented by orthodox belief, but I had found it impossible. Reason, or so it seemed to me, rejected the theme that God stepped into the earthly scene at a point of time in history and deliberately died as a man, and thereby, and from that time, saved sinners by his vicarious sacrifice. My reason boggled at the idea and my imagination could not encompass it. But George Fox's theme that the Creator had 'from the beginning' imparted something of himself to every person of his creation opened up a new approach to the whole question.

In particular it stimulated a new appreciation of the first chapter of the Fourth Gospel, rendering the philosophic concept of the *Logos*, the Word of God, the Greek principle of Reason and universal Law, into human, even homely terms, at the same time endowing this cold hellenistic theory with a human relevance and warmth. For while I had failed to accept the strange idea that God had chosen the date 4 B.C. (or was it 6 B.C.?) finally to reveal Himself, and Bethlehem as the site of His advent, I had little difficulty in accepting the 'Word made flesh' as the culminating point in a steadily evolving process; and Palestine as a suitable place wherein it should be manifested.

Thus, in what was not an entirely heretical manner, I was able to accept the idea of the Incarnation. It was not a clear apprehension I had gained, but a vivid impression of acceptable truth, a new way of looking at God and Christ and Man. Many years afterwards I came upon a perfect clarification and exposition of what I then dimly apprehended in William Temple's profound interpretation of the Fourth Gospel — *Readings in St John's Gospel*. I give it in full, together with his own illuminating translation from the Greek of the verses referred to, i.e. verses 9–13. George Fox and his friends would have agreed with every word. Their enemies and persecutors would undoubtedly have condemned the passage as heresy. So here we have the greatest and best of modern churchmen expressing with so much more precision the views of early Friends on the doctrine of the divine Light, but not perhaps giving it the central place it has occupied in Quaker thought. Here is what William Temple writes:

VERSES 9–13 : *There was the light, the true light, which enlighteneth every man, — coming into the world. In the world he was; and the world through his agency came into being; and the world did not recognize him. To his own he came; and his own people did not recognize him. But as many as received him, to them gave he the right to become children of God.*

'We now approach the new revelation. From the beginning the divine light has shone. Always it was coming into the world; always it enlightened every man alive in his reason and conscience. Every check on animal lust felt by the primitive savage, every stimulation to a nobler life, is God self-revealed within his soul. But God in self-revelation is the Divine Word, for precisely this is what that term means. What is constituted within that divine self-communication, as one element composing it, is the energy of Life; this is what urges all kinds of living things forward in their evolution; and this is what is fully and perfectly expressed in Christ. So it may be truly said that the conscience of the heathen man is the voice of Christ within him — though muffled by his ignorance. All that is noble in the non-Christian system of thought, or conduct, or worship is the work of Christ upon them and within them. By the Word of God — that is to say, by Jesus Christ — Isaiah, and Plato, and Zoroaster, and Buddha, and Confucius conceived and uttered such truths as they declared. There is only one divine light; and every man in his measure is enlightened by it.'

It would seem, according to this great Anglican Archbishop, that the unorthodox attempts of Penn to bring the heathen within salvation were not so wide of the mark.

In this identification of the Word of God through the ages with the fitful gleam from time to time manifested in the nobler strivings of men, both before and after Christ, we are confronted with a most satisfying view of man's relationship to God. In us there is a divine spark, a weak reflection of the Divine Light that shines through the evolutionary process that has made us men.

We are living participants in the life of a living God, related to Him as creature to Creator. We are vehicles of God's spirit, which is within us closer than breathing. This is so important. It removes the burden that weighs upon finite minds when they strive to comprehend and apprehend the absoluteness, unchangingness and remoteness, the coldness, of an Infinite Being beyond our knowing. As John William Graham has said, 'as thought moves on into such abstractions as this, it moves away from the human heart, and from the needs of men'.

Moreover, to believe that the fitful gleam making for a better life is the indwelling Christ at work in our personality, establishes also a new relationship with our fellow men. We become related to them through the common bond of our relationship to God. The acknowledgment of this relationship carries with it new responsibilities which defy neglect. Offences against our neighbour, or failure in neighbourly love, become offences against our own intrinsic nature, a deliberate obscuring of the Light in ourselves as we fail to respond to the Light of God in others. This theme of unity among men runs through the *Epistles* of George Fox as it does through many other Quaker writings. The indwelling Christ unifies, integrating personality and uniting persons:

'Friends and Brethren, the Eternal Word from which ye have both spoken and ministered to others, is the Word of Life, the Word of Peace, the Word of Reconciliation, which makes of Twain one New Man. . . . Therefore in the Light wait, where Unity is . . . where there is no Rent nor Division.'

Thus, in this unorthodox identification of the Logos with the Spirit of Christ at work through the ages, I had built up what was for me a satisfactory view of God's relationship to men. The error according to orthodox Christology was in identifying the Logos, or continuing Spirit of Christ through the ages, with the Holy Spirit, the Comforter, bestowed on the world by Christ after His death and resurrection. According to Christian orthodoxy, it is only the converted Christian who can receive the Holy Spirit, and it is true that Friends, both in the early days and today, while stressing verse 9 of the first chapter of St John's

Gospel —'the true light which lighteneth every man'— neglected verse 12 —'but as many as received him, to them gave he the light to become children of God'.* But we can forgive early Friends for a confusion of terms that has baffled theologians over many centuries. They had fastened onto a most productive growing point concerning the nature of man, when, with only the certainty of their own experience as evidence, they became convinced that in man there was a measure of the Light that was in Christ. For Fox to declare this in the face of current views of man's innate depravity was a heartening step in the direction of man's possible re-formation in the image of Christ.

If then, the prologue to the Fourth Gospel, as thus interpreted, seems to help us towards an understanding of the God-man relationship, how can it also help the unbeliever-who-wants-to-believe regarding the God-Christ relationship? I can only describe how the way opened for me.

The author of the Fourth Gospel brings to a single focal point the highest religious thought of the Greek and Hebrew worlds and presents us with the satisfying idea of an evolutionary spiritual progress through the ages, in which the Logos, the Word, the Light, the creating Spirit, is always at work. Through the prophets and sages, and in lesser degree in the lives of lesser men, this divine principle was steadily manifested in increasing measure, until, at a point of historical time propitious for the fullest revelation, God breaks through from the obscurity of the ages and expresses Himself as completely as He can be expressed in human form, in the man Jesus, whom we call Christ, the Son of God. The Word had become flesh and dwelt among us.

With a bold leap through centuries of controversy as to how the Divine Godhead could exist in the man Jesus, early Friends declared that they *knew* because they had experienced how the divine Light lived and worked in their own consciousness. The difference between Christ and themselves was the difference between the absolute and the relative. They had experienced a measure of the Spirit working in themselves and in other men; but to Christ, God had given the Spirit without measure and for

* See G. F. Nuttall, *The Holy Spirit in Puritan Faith and Experience*, for an elucidation of this point.

this reason He was in this unique way the Son of God. And because
Jesus possessed the Spirit in a complete degree, because His will
was therefore identical with God's will, He was indeed the Light
that enlighteneth every man. As Howard Brinton explains: 'like
the Hebrews, the Quakers usually thought in terms of will. They
knew from experience that sometimes their own wills were
united with God's will, that at other times their wills were opposed
to God's will. It was not difficult to go from that perception to
the realization that the will of Jesus was wholly the will of God,
not parallel to the will of God, but the very will of God'. Thus,
the uniqueness of Jesus does not rest on a supra-human or miraculous relationship with His Father, but on a complete identification
of His will with the will of His Father — 'not my will, but Thine,
be done'.

And in all this we discover the bond that unites God and
His perfect Son, and also the bond that unites both Father and
Son to us. The Word, the Light of Christ, comes from the
Eternal God who works through men in history; it was manifested
fully in the man Jesus, and demonstrated fully as Jesus worked
and loved and taught and died among men; it remains with us
after the Jesus of history dies in the act of willing surrender which
bears witness to the identity of the Holy Spirit within Him with
the same Spirit in men. His crucifixion was His final appeal on
earth to His own Spirit in men. Thus Christ continues His life in
us, making His home in the souls of men. And we are here faced
with the awful thought of the Divine Worker within us, the
indwelling Christ, who by a strange paradox is subject to our
own human will. For on us lies the responsibility of tending the
Seed, which will grow as we will it to grow. Our own experience
is enough to give us the assurance that human personality is
expansible, capable in small measure of creeping slowly towards
fulfilment.

Throughout their history there has been a tendency for some
Friends to sit loose to the historic Christ and to the historic
Incarnation. But was there not indeed a point in history when
God did reveal Himself in Jesus as He had not previously been
revealed in any man born of woman? I do not have to believe in
the Virgin Birth to believe that. Friends should face the fact that
it was the life and words of the historic Christ that had permeated

the consciousness of George Fox as a result of his incessant absorption with the New Testament. Fox found, as many of us today have found, an interpretation in the Fourth Gospel of the life and works and sayings of Jesus as recorded in Mark, Matthew and Luke. The author of the Fourth Gospel greatly enhances and expands the significance of the synoptic gospels. The special contribution of George Fox to our thinking is that it was from his inner experience that he discovered the truth the gospels told. The Fourth Gospel enables us to believe, in a way acceptable both to reason and to those apprehensions which are beyond reason, in the *contemporary* inspiration of the Holy Spirit and in the workings of this Spirit in human history. But more than this, if the Holy Spirit has worked and is still working in men's lives throughout historical time, then He will be working creatively in all the history that has yet to be made. And men are His only instruments. That is why it is so important for Christians to realize their responsibility as vehicles of the historically working Spirit, and why Friends should be a little less vague as to the scriptural origin of their belief in the Divine Seed.

This way of regarding the Person of Christ has the advantage of simplicity and seems also to explain, as far as can be explained, the mystery that surrounds his relationship to God and to man. I believe it is enough to go on with, sufficient to encourage us to waste no more time in demanding more explanation before we commit ourselves to His work as His servants. It is worth remembering that throughout the three centuries succeeding apostolic times the leaders of the ancient church stretched their brains and strained their tempers in vain attempts to achieve a neat logical structure that would explain the mystery of Father, Son and Holy Ghost. Ecumenical Councils met to decide the issue by discussion and vote, seldom achieving their object without sordid intrigue and the exercise of intolerant power against all heresy. Let us pause for a moment and consider whether these earlier controversies get us any further than the heresy of George Fox.

Among the earliest heresies was Docetism, whose supporters declared the human Jesus to be but a Phantom or Appearance, clothed in an unreal body, because God was too remote, transcendent, to feel or to suffer. In the second and third centuries the

Gnostics, serious rivals to the orthodox Christian, again stressed the remoteness of God, claiming that salvation came from knowledge (= Greek *gnosis*) of the lesser deities and emanations of God of whom Jesus was the chief. The Adoptionists, concerned that God should not be 'divided' into Father, Son and Holy Ghost because this idea was tainted with polytheism, taught that God adopted Jesus to explain God to men because he was such a good man. Such a view denies God's deliberate act in choosing to reveal Himself in Jesus. The Sabellians believed that the three Persons of the Trinity were not separate personalities but three 'modes' of expression in the one Personality. The Apollinarians deprive Christ of a human mind and spirit and declare him to be the *Logos* (Word) in a human body. The Nestorians conceived of Christ as two persons, one divine and one human: he was therefore capable of suffering and error in his human personality and could perform miracles by his divine personality. Arius, the protagonist of the great Arian heresy that rent the Christian world in the fourth century, declared God to be unknowable and unreachable, having no beginning and no end, that Christ was not eternal for he had a beginning, and as he was a Son he was therefore less than God. Hence Christ was not wholly God but part of God's creation.

Against all these heresies, each seeking for a definition of the relationship between God, Christ and men, the hierarchy of the Church set its face, and through its Councils eventually produced a definition that leaves us not greatly wiser except that all other conceptions of deity were condemned: Jesus Christ is declared to be of one essence with the Father, 'God from God, Light from Light, true God from true God, Begotten not created.'

The point of this diversion into ancient theological controversy is to indicate how desperately concerned Christians have been to gain a clear view of these God-Christ-Man relationships. The history of these attempts does not suggest that any logical system of thought gives the full answer. On the other hand, the convictions of early Friends, though founded on no persuasive logic, have a special value because they grow out of personal experience that distils sense out of much controversy.

Closely associated with this difficult conception of the Incarnation is the problem of the Resurrection. At the outset we must face the historical fact that Christianity was founded upon the experience of the Resurrection in the followers of Jesus. Nothing else can explain the beginning of Christianity. But the belief that the body of Jesus physically rose from the grave in a new physical life baffled and still baffles my credulity. I cannot see how it helps, and I confess I just do not know what really happened at the tomb. Moreover, I do not think it is important to know. This seems to be one of the points where Christianity can be a too materialistic religion. But what matters very much is the undoubted fact that after Christ's death there was a tremendous resurrection of power in His depressed disciples, due to the inflowing of the Holy Spirit into those who had for a few days failed to realize that the Christ did not die, could not die, with the human body of Jesus.

These dispirited men and women had experienced the resurrected 'spiritual body', or divine spirit, in their own hearts — and the rest followed. This is a miracle I can easily believe, because it has happened so often since, even if less splendidly than it happened then. It was by this Spirit that Paul was converted and through whose working that he was enabled to conquer the pagan world. Are not these sufficient reasons for claiming that after Christ's death the world can never be the same? Christ's death was an event in time; Christ Risen is a contemporary and continuing presence.

V

WHAT CANST THOU SAY?

'This is the great work of the scriptures, and their service to us, that we may witness them fulfilled in us, and so discern the stamp of God's Spirit and ways upon them, by the inward acquaintance we have with the same Spirit and work in our hearts.'

ROBERT BARCLAY

IT HAS BEEN SAID that 'though the Bible were lost it might be found in the mouth of George Fox'. This was a statement with little exaggeration in it. Fox and his followers were well acquainted with the Bible and became formidable debaters on the interpretation of the text. But, far more than they realized, they were so overwhelmed by the quickening experience of the Light in themselves that they too easily neglected the source from which their enlightenment came. As Neave Brayshaw has said, 'the radiant assurance of the inward teaching of the Spirit, caused them to minimize, or even forget, their indebtedness to the outward scripture for the first *suggestion* of the truths which they now realized were their own'. What had happened, of course, was that words imperfectly understood had been read and absorbed into their unconscious to re-appear in their conscious minds as part of their own inspiration. Neave Brayshaw recounts an experience of Samuel Bownas' who, when he was twenty years of age, began his first ministry with the words 'Fear not them which can kill the body but are not able to kill the soul.' Two years later he discovered that these were his Lord's own words and remarks 'No doubt I had read it, but had taken so little notice of what I read, it was to me as if it had never been writ.' This is a common experience. We tend only to accept consciously what seems at the time relevant to our need.

Friends' attitude to the Bible in the early days, and today, is yet another instance of their desire to get behind words and forms to the spiritual agency that gave them birth. Hence they believe the words of Scripture are important, but not more important than

41

the Spirit which inspired them. Barclay describes the written or 'outward' word as 'a declaration of the fountain and not the fountain itself, therefore they are not to be esteemed the principal ground of all truth and knowledge, nor yet the adequate primary rule of faith and manners'; they are rather to be subordinate to the Spirit 'from which they have all their excellency and certainty'. Thus Barclay gives to the Scriptures a secondary position to the Light that dwelt in the minds of the writers of the many and varying books of the Bible. That the 'outward Word' remains in a position of high authority, nevertheless, is indicated by his outright declaration that 'whatsoever any do, pretending to the Spirit, which is contrary to the Scriptures, is to be accounted and reckoned a delusion of the devil'. And as far as we can gather Fox never claims that the revelations of religious truth that came directly to him in any way superseded the teaching of the New Testament.

Quakerism, then, is not the religion of a Book but the religion of the Holy Spirit. Fox said that when God 'opened' to him that every man was enlightened by the Divine Light of Christ, he did not know 'where to find it in the Scriptures; though afterwards, searching the Scriptures, I found it. For I saw in that Light and Spirit which was before Scripture was given forth, that all must come to that Spirit, if they would know God, or Christ, or the Scriptures aright, which they that gave them forth were led and taught by'. Here again we see Fox probing behind words in search of the Spirit that inspired words. To know the Scriptures as a living source of power, penetrating and searching and guiding us in our daily living, we must share in the inspiration of their authors. Penington expresses this idea very well whan he says: 'We can truly say concerning the Scriptures that now we believe, not so much because of the relation of things concerning Christ which we have found in them, but because we have seen and received the thing which the Scriptures speak of.' What they had 'received' was the conviction that every man possessed the discerning Light that would make the word of Scripture evident in his life.

In his memorable sermon in Ulverstone Church, Fox asks the congregation to ask themselves whether their belief comes inwardly from God: 'You will say, Christ saith this and the

apostles say this, but what canst thou say?' The power of this
appeal impelled Margaret Fell to cry in bitter self-revealing 'we
are all thieves, we are all thieves; we have taken the Scriptures in
words and know nothing of them in ourselves'. This was the
crux of the matter, and still is, as far as Quakers are concerned.
What have we in ourselves that will reveal in all holy writing its
fullest meaning for us? Penn repeats the same theme: 'You
profess the Holy Scriptures, but what do you witness and experience? What interest have you in them? Can you set your seal
they are true by the work of the same Spirit in you that gave
them forth in the holy ancients?'

Let us take some familiar examples from the Bible to illustrate
what Friends meant by saying that it is so easy to accept the
'words' without 'knowing them' in ourselves. Micah, for instance,
requires us 'to do justly and to love mercy, and to walk humbly
with thy God'. In this injunction there are two ethical demands
and one appeal to establish a special kind of relationship with
God, or, according to Quaker interpretation, with the Holy
Spirit that spoke to Micah. Now we can accept these words —
justice, mercy — intellectually, purr in approval over them,
declare how fine and noble they are, and preach sermons on them.
But, say these early Friends, unless we experience as a total impact
on our whole personality the full meaning of what justice is so
that we become just men; unless mercy itself, not merely the
word-symbol that stands for the concept of mercy, becomes a
quality in our hearts that makes us merciful — then we do not
know what justice and mercy really are. Likewise, until we have
rid our hearts of pride and self-regard, until we have learned to
accept God's pattern for our lives rather than our own, until we
have been able to say 'not my will, but Thine, be done', and
mean it and act on it, then, although we may have conceived of
the nature of humility in an intellectual way, we have not translated the idea of humility into the state of being humble. To know
what humility is we have to be humble, and to recognize true
humility at work in another man. It was the flash of insight
resulting from Fox's challenge 'but what canst thou say?' that
impelled Margaret Fell humbly to declare that 'we are all thieves'.

Or, consider Jesus' brief commandment, 'Judge not,' tied up
with his demand that we should be less concerned with the mote in

our brother's eye than with the beam in our own eye. Here we are not asked to accept this test of our charitable attitude to other people by an approving admission that on the whole it is a good thing not to sit in judgment on others. We must get behind the words and subject ourselves to the discipline of resisting the easy tendency in all of us to compound for sins we are inclined to by damning those we have no mind to. We must examine our own sinfulness and ask ourselves by what right we sit in judgment on the sins of others. For our own shortcomings obscure our insights, and if neglected, blunt our perceptions and make all true judgment impossible. This obtuseness Jesus dubs with the disturbing word 'hypocrisy'. According then, to Quaker interpretation, we have not taken the 'Word' into ourselves until it has become a principle of action informing our conduct.

Next let us take an injunction from St Paul —'be bondservants one to another in love'. Here Paul is declaring the nature of the freedom of those who have faith in the efficacy of the Christ Spirit to lift them above the fleshly indulgences lying as obstacles across the path that the Christian must tread. Christ, he tells the Galatians, has freed them from the pointless observances of the old Law; they are now to live in a new dimension that gives them wide scope for expressing the Spirit of the newly found Christ in their hearts. But having thrown off the shackles of the rigid outward requirements of the Jewish Law, they must recognize the conditions for perpetuating their new freedom. He once again presents us with the Christian paradox — we are free only if we are bound. And the bond is service, the service in love that leads to freedom, because only by being bondservants to one another in love do we escape from the self that seeks its own indulgence. We 'bottom' the meaning of these words then, only when we have really loved our neighbour by an outgoing concern that establishes him and not ourselves as the primary object of our affections. We have not fully accepted our role as bondservant by agreeing that it is a good thing to love our neighbour or by declaring how true are these words of Paul; but only when they have become the spring of action in our relations with all men.

This, I think, is what early Friends were trying to say when they ask 'What canst thou say?' What can we witness? How far home into the still centre of our intelligence and imagination have the words penetrated? Francis Howgill, in a beautiful simplicity reminiscent of gospel wording, thus summarizes the intimate nature of this 'taking in' to ourselves of words which remain outside us, so to speak, until they have become part of our being, as an instinct is part of us:

'Why gad you abroad? Why trim you yourselves with the saints' words when you are ignorant of the life? Return, return to Him that is the first love, and the first-born of every creature, who is the Light of the world. . . . Return home to within; sweep your houses all, the groat is there, the little leaven is there, the grain of mustard-seed you will see, which the Kingdom of God is like. . . . Here you will see your Teacher not removed into a corner, but present when you are upon your beds and about your labour, convincing, instructing, leading, correcting, judging and giving peace to all that love and follow Him.'

But we must note one aspect of the attitude of early Friends to the Scriptures that was fraught with great danger. There were those among them who were so obsessed with their newly-found liberation of spirit, so convinced that they had been made free of the very mind of Christ, that they elevated above all authority the guidance of the Holy Spirit speaking in their own hearts. Here they fell into the error of most enthusiasts, believing in personal divine direction so absolutely as to accept all promptings of mind as the very word of God, and therefore, infallible. Hence many Friends went so far as to test the truth of Scripture by the spirit in themselves, rather than use the word of Scripture as the criterion for judging the validity of their own convictions. Believing that they possessed in themselves the same spirit that inspired the apostles, they could see no reason why their spiritual judgment was not the same as that of the apostles. They had made the mistake, so often made by the enthusiastic convert, of confusing the small Seed with the flourishing plant.

Some Friends of the first generation so lost sight of the biblical origin of their convictions and of the need to test personal guidance by scriptural principles, that they lapsed into the extravagances and gross individualism of the ranting sects on the extreme left of the Puritan movement. This neglect of a more sober and humble interpretation of their inner promptings called forth the condemnation of George Fox who had preserved a more balanced view of the relationship of the word of Scripture to the Inner Light. Another danger of Friend's attitude to the Bible has been a tendency, accentuated at certain periods in their history, to neglect its disciplined study as a source of nourishment to the mind as well as to the spirit. Here the effect was to restrict the channels of enlightenment to such direct intimations as came to individuals in the quiet of meditation. The result was an impoverishment of individual spiritual life among people who were content to regard themselves as 'the Lord's quiet ones'.

On the other hand, there was much gain in Friends' refusal to accept the Bible literally as the Word of God, equally true in all its contradictory parts and the sole arbiter of religious belief. Friends have never been 'Bible Christians': they set their faces against exchanging the authority of an infallible authoritarian church for the equally tyrannous authority of a Book. No matter how shaky the theological foundations of this refusal may seem to be, we can claim that Quakerism has never been associated with intolerance, although Quakers have been among the most persecuted of Christian sects. For this mercy we have reason to thank those pioneers who sat free to the tyranny of words and sought to found human relationships on love rather than on rigid conformity.

Again, with a tender logic following from their working hypothesis that God dwelt in men, and that His evolutionary purpose is revealed throughout human and cosmic history, Quakers find no difficulty in believing that God has never ceased to reveal Himself to men. The uniqueness of the special revelation in the New Testament is no reason for believing that it was a final revealing. This conviction has enabled Quakers to accept, without any disturbance of faith, any new truth concerning the evolution of the physical universe or the nature of man. Galileo, Newton, Darwin, Einstein, the findings of modern biblical criticism as well as those of modern psychology, can all be fitted comfortably into a faith that possesses the resilience to accept truth on any matter and from whatever quarter it may be revealed.

VI

MIND THAT WHICH IS PURE

Be ye perfect.
JESUS
Mind that which is pure in you to guide you to God.
GEORGE FOX

IF WE accept the working hypothesis that there is in man a quality of the divine akin to the Holy Spirit that was in Jesus, then we are led to ask these two questions: How does the Light operate? To what degree and by what means may we move in the direction of perfection? — or to put the question in homelier terms, what steps can ordinary people take to become better people? I shall attempt to answer these questions in a practical way, more by an appeal to our own human experience than by any logical deduction from theological propositions.

We can begin with the beautiful words of Fox's contemporary Edward Burrough: 'The divine mystery of the infinite God is revealed and discovered in the hearts of the sons of men whom he hath chosen; and he hath given us to enjoy and possess in us a measure of the fullness that is in Himself, even a measure of the same love and life, of the same mercy and power, and of the same divine nature. . . .' Now this does not mean that early Friends believed men to be born good. As far as I can gather from their lives and writings they were more conscious of the sinfulness of men than we are. They would have had little patience with the view that there is no need of religion to make men good because God had forestalled this necessity by making man in His image. Nothing in human experience can lead us to hold that man is fundamentally good. So optimistic a view should surely have received its death blow amidst the events of the twentieth century.

But there is a great difference between believing that man is fundamentally good and believing that there is something fundamentally good in man. This first generation of Friends were striking a blow against the gloomy doctrine of the total depravity of man, the dominant emphasis in the Calvinistic Protestantism of their day. And at the same time they pointed to a way of salvation from sin other than by the remote and miraculous intervention of God in Palestine centuries before. Fox's message was a denial of the doctrine that man is by nature wholly evil, but it was also the assertion of the good news that man's Saviour was not only crucified in history but was alive and potential in men's hearts today. He impelled bewildered minds towards the neglected miracle that Christ was in very deed living among them, not as a theological expression, not as a means of grace mediated through a priest, but as a giver of new life to sinful men, if only they dare to look into their own souls. He accepted quite literally, and with all its practical implications, Jesus' astonishing declaration that 'the Kingdom of God is within you'. Begin there, Fox says. And that is where we must begin.

There is no easy optimism in the Quaker view of life. Fox had no illusions about sin; but he asks us to deal with it in a new way. When early Friends likened God's gift to a 'Seed' they did not think of it as growing inevitably into a noble tree. They were fully aware of the influences that might arrest its growth. Fox never regarded the conquest of sin as a casual undertaking. But with astonishing psychological insight he laid the whole emphasis of his method not on the sin but on the light that revealed it. By implication he was criticising those who were so obsessed with the fallen state of man that they stayed their eyes on man's wickedness rather than on the means of his redemption. To contemplate evil is a poor way of becoming good. For as it is always true that we tend to go the way we are looking, it is sensible to look the way we want to go. So, we are to 'stand still in the Light and submit to it'. We are not to wait upon some miraculous event that we hope will change our lives through no effort of ours; rather are we to turn to the present miracle that Christ is waiting to perform daily in our lives. Fox assures his friends that Light will come on conditions. These conditions were well laid down by Isaac Penington in the darkness of Reading gaol: 'We were directed to search for the least of all seeds and to mind the lowest appearance thereof, which was its turning against sin and darkness, and so, by minding and observing that in us which turned against sin and darkness, we came by degrees to find we had met with the pure living, eternal Spirit.'

The practice of minding 'the lowest appearance' of the Seed involves a steady discipline. We must face the austerity as well as accept the joy of life if we are to grow. The method of this discipline is beautifully and most practically suggested in George Fox's oft-repeated instruction 'Mind that which is pure in you to guide you to God.' Here Fox displays a deep psychological insight, born of his own personal struggle. We are to use the little that we have to make it more. We are to tend the small Seed and help it to grow. It is the scientific method applied to religion. Every scientist uses it; every saint has practised it. This method can rightly be called also the method of faith, if we can conceive of faith not as a bundle of beliefs that we have to accept before we can act, nor as a capacity to believe in the improbable or an acceptance of beliefs others say are true, but as a practical means of discovering truth by experimenting with possibilities and probabilities based on truths we already possess.

In any honest attempts to discover new truth, there are two methods open to us: we can either refuse to accept as true everything that has not yet been proved to be true; or we can begin by assuming to be true what has not yet been proved to be untrue. St Paul, George Fox, the saints throughout the ages and the modern scientist commend the latter course. The discipline proceeds something like this: We are faced with a choice between two decisions, each of which will demand action, but one of which will leave us comfortably where we are, although perhaps with a regret that we have not faced the music; the other will demand that we take a step into the uncomfortable unknown, because we know that, as far as we can see, it is the right decision to make. This sense of the rightness of the second line of action is the Light at work revealing the true way; it is 'that which is pure' stirring us out of our complacency. The method demands that we commit ourselves to the line of action that is prompted by this stirring of our better self.

By thus committing ourselves we step out of doubt into decision. This is a step in the right direction even though the grounds for our decision be imperfectly understood. But as the process goes on we shall gain assurance, one way or the other, by intermittent but accumulating glimpses of truth which will emerge in proportion as we have faithfully acted on the assumption that they are true. Each glimpse will reveal but a short distance of the way. It is, indeed, given to few men to experience a vast opening up of country in one moment of time. We succeed if we are good stayers. For most of us it can be no more than a step by step affair, into a darkness that becomes less dark if our steps are in the right direction. Even wrong action, that is action that results from a wrong assumption, is better than no action at all; for knowing where we go wrong is often as important as knowing where we are right. A step in the wrong direction helps us negatively; a step on the right way assists us positively. For practice in learning to believe is the way of experiment. In the end faith is an acted thing.

This scientific approach to reality is wonderfully described by von Hügel. He first draws an analogy from Darwin's researches, saying of him:

He was always learning, loving, watching, he was always 'out of himself', doubling himself up, as it were, so as to penetrate these realities so much lower than himself. He had never done and finished; what he learnt today had to be re-learnt . . . yet always with the same sense that what he had learnt was not his own mind and its fancies and theories, but realities and their real qualities and habits. His life thus moved out into other lives. And what he discovered was not clear but vivid; not simple but rich; not readily, irresistibly transferable to other minds, but only acquirable by them through a slow purification and a humble, loving observation and docility like his own.

Von Hügel then asks us to apply this loving, patient method to our own search for reality:

'We get to know such realities slowly, laboriously, intermittently, partially; we get to know them, not inevitably nor altogether apart from our dispositions, but only if we are sufficiently humble to welcome them, and sufficiently generous to pay the price continuously. . . . We get to know realities in proportion as we become worthy to know them, in proportion as we become less self-occupied, less self-centred, more outward moving, more lost in the crowd, more rich in giving all we have. . . . And we get to know that we know these realities by finding our knowledge . . . approving itself to us as fruitful . . . and all this in a thoroughly living and practical, in a concrete, not abstract, not, foretellable, in a quite inexhaustible way.'

Implicit, then, in the concept of the Seed as the central core of reality in man's nature is the concept of *growth*. This concept applies both to our gradual attainment of religious faith and also to the gradual maturing of our personality through right thinking and right living. And closely bound-up with the idea of growing into faith, of creeping slowly into the person we were intended to become, is the idea already referred to — the paradox that the Inner Light is in some sense subject to our will. It is subject to our will in the sense that by our own decision we may think and act in ways which will gradually allow the Light within us to glow into a steady flame and thus increasingly illuminate our way. This may happen until we become so habituated as it were, to making our responses faithfully to the highest degree of under-standing we at any time possess, that we make increasing progress towards thinking and acting in conformity with our guidance. And more than this; we find these right responses becoming easier to make, until in the end we may make them not only with less effort but even unconsciously, automatically. When this happens we have built up a solid foundation of character and faith.

When Jesus said 'Be ye perfect', that is, complete, integrated, mature, he was not asking the impossible. His startling injunction was founded on his knowledge of human capacity to respond to the Divine Seed of perfection that he knew to be inborn in men. His life and death were not gambles on the chance that this might be true, but demonstrations of his certainty that it was. It may be difficult to believe, but I believe it to be true, that most men and women for brief odd moments of their lives have achieved perfection. Maybe only for a split second, they have been out of their selves and inside other selves in an act of selfless abnegation. They have loved absolutely. And that is perfection. Amidst the tawdry futility of our lives, encumbered as they are with self-seeking and moral defeat, it is good to hold fast to this proven capacity of men to touch perfection — for brief moments and on rare occasions.

It will have been noted that Von Hügel's advice does not ask us to wait in aimless vacancy for something to happen to us by the grace of God. We are to become less self-occupied, more outward moving, more rich in giving. We are to live and think and adventure and pray in a definite and practical way. Paul's Damascus vision did not come out of the blue, sudden and miraculous as it seemed to be. He had looked into the eyes of the martyred Stephen, battling with their appeal as he breathed threats and slaughter on the followers of the Risen Christ. In the end his pride broke before the hated truth that assailed him. It was travail and thinking that prepared the way for the vision, which was, in effect, Christ breaking through from within, flooding his conscious self with a great light. And recognizing this 'true light that enlighteneth every man' he focused on it all his energies, capacities, thoughts, imaginations, and became a bondservant of the Crucified. In our humble way, too, we have to let the indwelling Christ break through; but we shall do well not to expect more than feeble intimations that this is happening. Paul was a religious genius; most of us have been cast in smaller moulds. Nevertheless, we are made of the same stuff.

But how shall we know that our Light is not darkness? Here, as we have seen, there lies a grave danger — the danger that we may be led to believe that every idea that comes into our heads comes from the true Light. This is a particular peril for those who are not convinced of the super-natural nature of the Light. This Light is from God, not to be identified with stray thoughts emerging into consciousness in moments of vacancy or effortless rumination. We lose the deeper note of the Quaker faith if we think that our ideas are God-given because they stir our consciousness with a sense of urgency. We have to be sure that they do not emerge from a murky sub-conscious. To be cocksure is not always to be right. Even our most violent enthusiasms, perhaps these in particular, have in some way to be laid with humility before the judgment seat of Christ, to be subjected to his searching

Light, tested with his values, so that our mind gets as near, as in its frailty it can, to His mind.

There are two main ways of testing the quality of our promptings. The first way is to share our 'openings' with others who have gone further than we have in Christian discipline and wisdom. The second way is to examine our leadings in the light of gospel teaching. The more we study the gospels the more firmly we shall grasp the essential nature of the values Jesus stressed. But intensive reading of essential passages is more important than extensive reading that does not bite into our minds. One of the simplest ways to get at the mind of Christ is to concentrate on His parables, on the Sermon on the Mount and on His way of reacting to men and women when they faced Him with a problem in human conduct. In this simple study we shall find Him exercising an unerring perception of motive and a consistently healing and re-building power. We shall learn what love in action looks like; the trustingness of it, the startling reversals of our own values that love demands. In Matthew, Mark and Luke we shall discover how Jesus worked; in the Fourth Gospel we shall learn who He was.

Into this reading we must put every ounce of sincerity and sensitiveness we possess. We must rid ourselves of pre-conceptions that inhibit understanding, and of ingrained thought-habits that have been built into our personalities by faulty education. social conditioning or class prejudice. In humility, we must attempt to assess the undertones of our daily living with the values we find emphasized in our reading; so that we are enabled to discover what counts most highly in Christ's eyes and what counts most in our own. This sensitivity to values requires of us a delicate awareness of our motives and attitudes, so that we may recognize our thought-habits for exactly what they are. Why, for instance, do we hold the views about men, conduct, social justice, that we do hold? For truth's sake or for comfort's sake? The Light in us guided by the Light we see at work in the gospels will tell us. It will help us to discern the difference between spiritual pride and good will; between self-complacency and humility; between a just decision and a self-interested one. And it will help us to perceive the close similarity between the sins we are inclined to and sins we have no mind to. For one of the first works of the true Light in us is to develop our capacity to distinguish between the false currency of a mean life and the coinage of generous living. It is by attending to these rudiments of the good life that we begin our quest for a steady faith in the living Christ. We begin to realize that faith is not necessarily the point from which we begin but the end of the journey. And yet not the end of our journey, for the adventures of faith set us on many journeys, in each of which we find the knowledge gained 'approving itself to us as fruitful'.

VII

CANDLE AND LANTHORN

'Conscience is an excellent thing, where it is rightly informed and enlightened; wherefore some of us have fitly compared it to the lanthorn, and the light of Christ to a candle: a lanthorn is useful when a clear candle burns and shines in it; but otherwise of no use.'
ROBERT BARCLAY

ARE NOT Friends confusing the Light of Christ in the human soul with what we call conscience? We can best answer this question by considering what our conscience is and how it is formed. The crudest view regards conscience as an inborn capacity to judge between right and wrong. On this assumption we should expect the views of right and wrong held by different men to be at least similar if not identical. But even our own limited experience of conscientious conflict between men reveals that individual views of right and wrong differ greatly. When we glance backwards over human history we find that thousands of God-fearing men have conscientiously persecuted other equally God-fearing men who themselves have gone to the scaffold or to the stake or faced the firing squad for conscience sake. Persecution, burnings and cruel intolerance, slavery and racial prejudice, the more subtle injustices inflicted by class pride and economic theory, are samples of evils arising out of a clear conscience. There can be no doubt that Hitler and Stalin were obeying their consciences when they liquidated their enemies. When we come closer home to examine our own frailties we find ourselves harbouring unworthy thoughts and performing acts of doubtful quality with little or no conscientious scruple. Such reflections suggest that what we call conscience is by no means an infallible guide to righteous behaviour. If conscience is independent of tradition, education and social environment, if it is a fully equipped 'faculty' of our personality, then why does conscience operate in so many conflicting ways in different men, and differently in the same men at different times?

The answer is clear. Our conscience is not a perfectly fashioned instrument presented to us at birth as part of our natural endowment. It is the product of our upbringing, of all the formative influences, good and evil, that slowly make us the men and women we are. This is why the magistrate who tells the young offender of tender years that 'he ought to know the difference between right and wrong' is talking nonsense. A child's knowledge of right and wrong depends almost entirely on what his parents and teachers have taught him, especially by their example. Hence the most we can say about our conscience is that it is a *capacity within us* to be educated for discerning the difference between right and wrong. If our teacher is a Fagin then we shall have an easy conscience about stealing; if a communist commissar then, perhaps, easy views about the relativity of social conduct; if the only impact on our judgment comes from men engaged entirely in the jungle warfare of acquiring worldly goods, our conscience will happily agree that the devil may take the hindmost; but — and here we come to the heart of the matter — if we are submitted, and submit ourselves, to the Spirit of Christ speaking within us, then we shall have an educated Christian conscience.

Read again the words of Robert Barclay at the head of this chapter. His delightful simile of the candle and the lantern exactly explains the relation of the Light of Christ to conscience. The lantern is not the Light; the candle is the Light, shining dimly or brightly, within the lantern, which is the human personality through which the Light shines. This Light forms our judgments, for, as Barclay says, 'Conscience followeth the Judgments, doth not inform it.' The Light, he continues, 'removes the blindness of the Judgment, opens the Understanding, and rectifies both the Judgment and Conscience'. The fallible conscience is never enough; it is our life's task to 'mind that which is pure' so that step by step we approach nearer to the truly educated Christian conscience. Then we shall find life very exciting, very rewarding and sometimes very awkward.

Thus our conscience is an end-product of a very complicated set of circumstances. It grows as our character grows; it is never a perfect instrument; it is always being made. Our parents, our family life, our teachers, the social, national, racial and religious groups to which we belong, all play their part. Inherited traditions and present experience, our personal endowments and peculiarities of temperament, have their influence in its formation. But within these limitations there is a wide scope for the personal disciplines that enable us to form our own conscience. And this is where successive acts of will, faithful obedience to the Light within, consistent testing of our values by Christ's values, gradually moulds our conscience into conformity with Christian values. When this has happened, even imperfectly, conscience does indeed become the deepest self rising into consciousness, asserting itself as a true guide to judgment and action; the self that boldly voices and practices its ideals, controlling passion and mean impulse that impede the operation of the educated Christian conscience.

The main obstacles to the proper working of conscience are unexamined enthusiasms, inert ideas and the intrusion of self. Enthusiasms untested by Christian standards lead us into futile extravagances and harmful intolerance that destroy rather than create, divide rather than unite. We especially have to examine our motives — is our enthusiasm founded on love or envy? Inert ideas, that is, the unexamined opinions that determine so much of our thinking, must be brought under the ruthless rays of the candle in the lantern, which will reveal whether they are a relic of that spiritual obtuseness in complacent men that called forth Jesus' condemnation. The Light, Barclay reminds us, removes such blindness, opens up the channels of understanding and rectifies, straightens out, the conscience. Lastly, the most obstinate barrier, is concern centred on self. Here we have the common cause of misdirected 'conscientious' action. When our conscience remains ego-centric, our decisions will be self-regarding, tied up with the insistent demand that the primary factor in our judgment is 'how will this affect me?' But, obviously, as all our judgments and decisions affect other people, the educated Christian conscience requires that our major concern should be how our decision affects them. Conscience should never supersede the truth to which it has to testify.

The Light of Christ within the human personality is not, therefore, to be confused with the imperfect human conscience struggling, through failure and success, to become a worthy judgment-forming influence in our lives.

VIII

ANSWERING THAT OF GOD

'Be patterns, be examples in all countries, places, islands, nations, wherever you come, that your carriage and life may preach among all sorts of people, and to them; then you will come to walk cheerfully over the world, answering that of God in every one.'

GEORGE FOX

'There is no failure except the failure of the imagination.'

CHARLES MORGAN

IT IS NOT enough to 'return home to within' if the Seed is to flourish. We have also to turn outwards to the world about us. Christ always works in a social situation. For the Light is an active principle which liberates personality by transforming self-regarding sentiments into other-regarding sentiments. Slowly the object of our love is changed from our selves to our neighbour through God. This process, long and never fully perfected in men, gradually integrates our personality by focusing self on worthy objects beyond our self. Thus man becomes himself in his out-going to others —'he that loseth his life shall save it'. And in this way he is in a real sense re-born.

But to be thus re-born comes not by intellectual acceptance of a creed. Knowing is not being or doing. When we stand shivering beside our cold bath on a chilly morning and say 'Smith, be a man', we have not thereby achieved manliness. When we admit love of our neighbour through God to be our highest good, we have not yet loved our neighbour. Love is not in control until we have become active on behalf of our neighbour. And we cannot become active in any useful way if any part of our thinking is shot through with self-interests, unexamined traditions and thought-habits that predetermine our attitude to our neighbour, and sometimes obscure our knowledge even of his existence. It is at this point that we have to recognize two special aspects of the Inner Light which have direct bearing on good living.

We remember, that the test for our understanding of how the true Light works is the witness of Jesus at work. In the Gospels we find the active principle of love supported by Jesus' superb intelligence and imagination. We can only conclude, therefore, that if we wish to have the mind of Christ we must exercise our intelligence within the field of our imagination. To be sensitive to the world of suffering and to have no means of healing; to feel the cruelties of human selfishness and pride and to see no way of softening them beyond little acts of kindness and of love, drives the sensitive soul to despair. We have not only to be aware of evil, we have to diagnose and deal with it. This can be done partly by that expression of God's will we call intelligence. Thinking thus becomes a moral duty.

One of the difficulties of our time is not that there are so many wicked men about but that the children of this world are so often wiser than the children of light. This was also the problem of Jesus in His day. The 'good' are so frequently stupid, and the wicked usually so clever. Jesus condemned sin but He was charitable to sinners. The only people for whom He reserved His most bitter condemnation were the spiritually obtuse, which also means the unimaginative, those who did not see, but who ought to have seen, the moral and social obligations of the religion they professed. Judged by the conventions of their age those whom Jesus condemned were good men. They conformed rigidly to the Law; they were eminently respectable. But the rigidity of their rules held their imagination in thrall, and it was for this that Jesus called them hypocrites, the most accusatory word in his vocabulary.

For it is imagination that bridges the gap between man and man. Without this 'living power and prime agent of all human perception', effective love remains crippled. Imagination is 'a repetition in the finite mind of the eternal act of creation . . . it is essentially *vital*'. Coleridge is writing of the poetic imagination, but how well his definition describes the social imagination that enables us to get inside other people's skins, thinking, feeling and suffering with them in vital sympathy. It is imagination thus defined that impels Fox's realization that he must 'have a sense of all conditions' if he is to 'speak to all conditions'. Perhaps nowhere in Quaker annals has this divine quality been more richly demonstrated than in John Woolman's decision in 1763 to visit the savages in the Pennsylvanian forests that 'I might feel and understand their life and the spirit they live in, if haply I might receive some instruction from them.' For here he witnesses to the peculiar humility essential for the reception of the truth that imaginative perception reveals. Imagination is the eyes of Love; it is outreaching, seeing beyond the obvious to the possible, transforming enemies into friends, sinners into penitents. To have imagination is the condition of success if we are to walk over the earth 'answering that of God in everyone'.

This need for identification with human suffering that only imagination makes possible is a constant theme in the lives of Fox and Woolman. A Friend wrote of Fox during his illness in the Barbados 'he bears the iniquity wherever he comes'. John Woolman speaks of his vision of 'human beings in as great misery as they could be and live, and that I was mixed with them, and that henceforth I might not consider myself as a distinct or separate being'. And during his last illness he reflects how 'I felt the misery of my fellow creatures separated from the divine harmony, and it was heavier than I could bear.' These faithful children of the Light were always seeking to be *within* the souls of others, an exercise which Fox describes as having a 'sense' of their condition, or, in a phrase of broader meaning, as having 'unity with the creation'. The Bantu proverb 'Man is other Men' expresses this sense of human relationship in another way, and with what poignant relevance in these days of Africa's crisis!

George Fox's injunction that we should go about our daily lives 'answering that of God' in all men follows inevitably from the central Quaker emphasis on the indwelling Christ. The logic is simple but profound. If we believe that every man has in him the capacity for response to the appeal of our love for him then it is to that capacity alone we must 'speak'. It is a two-way traffic, therefore; 'that of God' in us must respond to and appeal to 'that of God' in our neighbour. In situations of conflict we do not attempt to dominate his mind or to use physical force; we assume the most reconciling attitude and seek for the growing point of creative agreement. Because men are temples of the Holy Spirit we respect to the uttermost the sanctity of human personality;

seeking only to heal and to save, never to avenge or condemn. We are allowed to hate cruelty and meanness but we must love the cruel and the mean; we must learn to love those who hurt us; and, a more difficult thing to do, we must learn to love those who hurt others.

When we observe Jesus at work this is the principle we find in operation. He 'speaks' to that of God in the sinner and heals him; he accepts the oil of spikenard in recognition of a sinner's capacity to give without restraint; when the prodigal is 'yet afar off' the Father goes out to meet him with only the desire for restoration in his heart, the memory of his wayward son's betrayal cast aside as an irrelevance. Perhaps the most superb instance of answering 'that of God' recorded in the Gospels is the incident of the woman taken in adultery (John VIII). Here is a situation tense with conflict, seemingly fated to end in horrible cruelty for the satisfaction of customary law, but in no change of heart either in accusers or accused. Picture the scene: the hard-minded elders bent on 'justice' and on trapping Jesus in the meshes of the Law; the sinning woman facing a death as agonizing as crucifixion; Jesus in the midst. The fact of guilt is not at issue; the woman was taken 'in the very act'. Nor is there any doubt about the legal penalty: the law of Moses 'commanded us to stone such'. 'What then sayest thou?', ask the upholders of the Law.

Jesus said nothing. He waited, holding the situation in suspense; and then he breaks the expectant silence with words that raised the whole situation on to another plane. The elders had asked the wrong question; Jesus prompts them to ask the right one —'He that is without sin among you, let him cast the first stone.' The centre of the conflict now recedes from the visible scene into the hearts of the accusers. Something quite new has penetrated into these minds set hard in tradition. The scribe who added the gloss retained in our Authorized Version, 'being convicted of their own conscience', knew what had happened. Again Jesus waits for the leaven to work; until the accusers retreat one by one, leaving the woman alone, before Christ. He has answered 'that of God' in her accusers with a stern appeal to a new way of thinking. His appeal to the woman is quite different. 'Hath no man condemned thee?' 'No man, Lord.' And while condemning her sin he trusts the healing power of divine compassion to work within her: 'Neither do I condemn thee: go, and sin no more.'

Here, then, is the perfect sample of a perfect response. It is not possible to conceive of any more creative release of what seemed to be a quite intractable human coil. To my mind, the importance of such a miracle far transcends in importance the nature miracles which worry the rational mind. Here Jesus 'speaks' to that puny Seed of divine origin buried deep even in the legalist and in the sinner. He seeks for the growing point of a changed mind, and trusts its power to grow. It is a grave risk He takes; but He knows what He is doing. He transforms an ideally bad situation into an ideally good situation by laying the emphasis on all the good that fitfully exists in the persons concerned in it. And this is what George Fox suggests we should do in our own encounters with human frailty.

This view of the Christian manner of response has informed the attitude of Friends to all personal and social and international situations. In theory at least, but I fear not always in practice, it has governed their views on private relationship between persons, on the conduct of business meetings, on the problems of peace and war, on race relations, penal reform, education and the whole area of social service. To these applications of the doctrine of the Inner Light we shall return later.

PART II

Implications

IX

PRAYER

'Ask, and it shall be given you; seek, and ye shall find; knock, and it shall be opened to you. . . . If ye then, being evil, know how to give good gifts unto your children, how much more shall your heavenly Father give the Holy Spirit to them that ask him.'

MATTHEW VII, 7–11

'Petitional prayer is only one department of prayer; and if we take the word in the wider sense as meaning every kind of inward communion or conversation with the power recognized as divine, we can easily see that scientific criticism leaves it untouched.'

WILLIAM JAMES

A. THE INEVITABILITY OF PRAYER

THROUGHOUT the ages, in every race, in all religions and in all parts of the earth, prayer has been a common practice of mankind. This universal practice of prayer is not a reason for accepting its necessity or efficacy, for there are many characteristics common to men that we could well do without. Throughout history men have been cruel, deceitful and selfish, but no one desires that they should continue so. And there are kinds of prayer that do not commend themselves either to our reason or to our charity. When, for instance, priests of warring nations pray to the same God for victory, even our sense of humour intervenes to suggest some confusion of thought; and prayers for success in business or for fine weather seem to lack a measure of proportion. If we are to discover whether prayer has any value, which means, also, whether men should pray, we have to seek the answer along quite other lines of thought. First we have to assume that there is a God. For the purpose of this chapter that hypothesis is accepted. Next we have to know whether or not we can establish communication with our God; and finally we have to show that this communication — prayer — is effective. This last suggestion I offer with some hesitation as there are some Christians whom I deeply respect who declare that prayer is an end in itself; just as love is an end in itself. This is a view I find it difficult to accept, for I prefer to regard even love as a means, the highest means, of producing the right results. In this sense prayer too is a means of achieving the right kind of religion and the right relationship with God and with men.

If we think carefully, even logically, about the God-man relationship which the Christian faith implies, we are bound to conclude that prayer is the most obvious, the altogether inevitable and central activity of religion. If we believe that to God we owe our being, that He is our Creator as we are His creatures, that He is the energizing and directing power of the spiritual universe, that we are His pale image, that we possess as men a quality that is part of Him, then the most obvious thing in all this complexity of relationships is that we should want to get into touch with Him. This is the one inescapable and logical deduction from our condition of incompleteness and dependence. There is no great virtue in independence if by this we mean a cocksureness that we are managing our own lives very well without the help of God or man. The man who thinks he lives his life independently of other men is a pathetic self-deceiver. No man can either eat, work, sleep or think in a permanent state of independence. Paradoxically enough the recognition of our incompleteness and dependence is a condition of our moral and physical growth. Since, then, it is the central theme of Christianity that men cannot progress towards completeness, or spiritual maturity, without divine assistance, it follows that 'communication with the power that is recognized as divine' becomes the primary method of growing in the right direction.

This argument, of course, is applicable only to those who belong to one of the great world religions in which this relationship of man to his Creator holds a central place. It is not for Christians to assume that Buddhism, Hinduism, Judaism and Islam have no contribution to make to our thinking about prayer. The Christian who sits at the feet of Gandhi or Tagore will learn much to his profit. But we are here concerned with those who call themselves Christians and with those who want to believe that Christianity is true. The importance of communication 'with the power recognized as divine' will receive small recognition from those who regard God as a philosophical abstraction or as a Father-projection of the unconscious mind. But if we accept religion as a primal need of men, then prayer becomes a vital act by which the whole human personality seeks its growth in the Source from which it draws its life.

B. TO WHOM WE PRAY

Nevertheless, we need to know more about 'the power recognized as divine' if we are to pray with any sense of security and trust. We cannot pray to a Life-Force, or to a First Cause, or to the *élan vital*, to an Absolute or to an It. Being persons we can only pray to a Him, to a being to whom we can ascribe *personality*, in some way not entirely dissimilar from our own personality. But the difficulty is that the average thinking man finds it more than baffling to conceive of the Power responsible for creating the infinite material universe as a Person. To describe this Creative Force as a Person seems to depart from the very meaning of personality as human beings think of it. A Mathematical Intelligence may be; even an Atomic Organizer; but as He — this is impossible to imagine except in the crudest metaphor. For personality conceived in human terms seems limited, finite, encompassable, small, utterly dissociated from the immense creative forces of our timeless, limitless universe. How, then, can we attribute to this immensity of Power behind things any kind of personality that even remotely resembles the most superb manifestation of human personality? The difficulty is real and not easily overcome.

It is possible to present arguments for a personal God, but no one of them is satisfactory. Nevertheless I give here an argument that I have found helpful in taking me part of the way. It has enabled me at least to see that the reasons for believing in a divine Personality are as good as those for not believing. They are based on B. H. Streeter's work *Reality*, one of the most bracing books on Christian faith written between the two wars.

The argument for a personal God takes us along two converging paths. We start first with ourselves. We know roughly what personality is when we apply the word to men and women, and we are bound to note an immense range of human personality varying between great richness and littleness. Then let us turn to our dog. Any dog-lover will undoubtedly attribute personality to his dog, and will know the many varying types of personality among the dogs he knows. But when he compares the personality of his dog to the personality of his wife, he is bound to admit a vast difference in scale. The personality he ascribes to his dog is so much more limited than that he can attribute to his wife. And if he keeps rabbits he will accord a far richer personality to his dog than to them. And so on. By going *down* the scale the 'quantity' of personality diminishes. But suppose from man we go *up* the scale. Suppose we think of the most superb spiritual quality of, say, men like St Francis or Gandhi, and then conceive of this quality immeasurably more complete and creative — Can we then begin to conceive of the It becoming He?

The difficulty at this point consists in the fact that so indefinite an enlargement of the concept of personality empties its usual meaning of any significance. It would not seem to matter much whether we call the Creative-Force He or It, because both are infinite, and therefore beyond our comprehension.

But, the argument continues, so far we have been discussing size, quanity. By doing so we remain oppressed by the immensity of the universe and the infinity of It. But we must realize that the essence of personality is not size or quantity but *intensity* and *quality*. The material of religion is the Spirit; the essence of a man is his spiritual life, not his body. Once grasp the point, says Streeter 'that personality and its characteristics are a matter of quality, not of quantity, and we can brave that astronomical intimidation to which otherwise from the mere size of the material universe we might succumb'. Do we not by this argument at least come to the conclusion that it is not fatuous to personify the Creator or to regard Him as the infinite self-consistent Source, free from all caprice and limitation, of the limited qualities of human kind?

Even so there still remains the danger which mankind seldom seems to avoid, and of which men must always be aware. This is the danger of operating our belief in the reverse direction, of assuming that, because we reflect some aspects of the nature of God, God reflects some aspects of the natural man. We must be careful to remember that we are the image in the mirror, a pale and imperfect image of the divine. Otherwise we shall fall into the abyss which has engulfed men throughout the ages, and still does — the danger of making God in our own image. To this anthropomorphic (man-shaped) view of God we can attribute every cruelty and foolishness committed in the name of religion — human sacrifice, the rack and the stake, wars and national pride, not to mention the superstitions of the ignorant and the smugness of the conventional. To personify the It with human vices is as easy as to endow God with human virtues. There is only one way to avoid making God in our own or in the racial image. This is to conceive of the Personality behind things in terms of the most satisfying portrait of God we possess. And that is Jesus Christ. Even if the outlines of this portrait are partially obscured by history, and by our own dim vision, it still remains the least unworthy portrait of the *quality* of God, the Person whom Jesus could best describe to us by the word Father.

To argue thus in support of the Christian belief that God is a Person is not to prove the truth of such a belief. The most such argument can do consists in helping us to believe that our belief is not foolish, that it is at least as sensible and satisfying as any other view of the Power behind things. But it can never be enough merely to argue ourselves through to a belief in a personal God. This has never been satisfactorily done, and is not likely to be. Every argument for the existence of a personal God has failed so far through some fallacy inherent in the reasoning. And so, to what amounts to no more than a tentative indication that we are on the right track, we have to add our own trust in such evidences of a personal God as we find in our own experience and in history. By far the most impressive of these signs is the life and death of Jesus. Does that give us confidence? If we found our belief on logic we shall probably end in unbelief; but if we look searchingly into the words and personality of Jesus we shall perhaps find there a more believable authority than the arguments of philosophers. We are not asked to pass an examination in logic; we are asked to look at divine Personality portrayed in a Life and in a historical Person. To believe what Christ believed, we may reasonably say, should be good enough for us.

It is not very satisfying to address our prayers to an unknown

God; we must have some idea of what He is like, of the kind of relationship we may reasonably assume between Him and us, and also of His purpose for us. By summing up God's nature in the word 'Father' Jesus fastens on the idea most easily comprehensible by ordinary men and women. God is a Person who cares, who is approachable, who has authority, who listens but also demands. These are all terms used to describe human persons and therefore limited in meaning when applied to God, as is the word 'Father' also. But we have more than words to help us. We have a Life which immensely extends the idea of 'Father' and enables us to understand the infinity of Love which is God. To this personified infinity of Love we pray, carrying in the background of our minds a picture of Love active among men in the life of Christ. This picture helps to project us out of vagueness into concreteness, out of a futile and purposeless sensation of words only into the activity which is Love.

C. THE NATURE OF PRAYER

Traherne has said of Christ that 'if he might have had but one request of God Almighty it should have been, above all other, that he might be a blessing to mankind . . . for he that is a blessing to mankind must be blessed'. This is the way that Jesus made Love active. His prayers were never a mere sinking back into contemplation of a sublime Divinity, but were always related to his service of Love among men. The nineteenth-century Russian priest, John of Cronstadt, explains why this must be so: 'Why, he asks, has our sincere prayer for each other such great power over others? Because of the fact that by cleaving to God through prayer I become one spirit with Him, and unite with myself, by faith and love, those for whom I pray; for the Holy Ghost acting in me also acts at the same time in them.' Thus prayer is never complete until we have united ourselves not only to God but also to our neighbour.

The scope of prayer is clearly outlined for us in the Lord's Prayer, which was an answer to the specific appeal, 'Lord, teach us to pray.' This simple but most comprehensive prayer embraces the worshipper's recognition of God as Father; the first act of adoration which releases us from self; our Christian responsibility for the spreading of God's Kingdom; the needs of our bodies; our relationship with our fellow men; the exercise of forgiveness and the recognition of our struggle with temptation and evil. This is all a man has to deal with — God, himself and his neighbour. Notice also not only the scope but the precision of this prayer. There is nothing vague or sentimental in it. It is a declaration that the Christian gospel ceases to function except in a concrete situation. Examine any occasion on which a prayer of Jesus is recorded in the Gospels and we shall find it was always related to a social situation —'for *their sakes* I sanctify myself'. But to say that prayer always deals with a concrete situation does not mean that we have only to present concrete problems to God for His solution. We have to present *ourselves* to God, so that we become persons who can deal with life in His way. Sanctification involves a purification of motive, a will energized and clarified. To sanctify our minds we have, therefore, to submit them in the quiet of the prayer-state to the inflowing of the divine Will. And then,

> 'All shall be well
> And all manner of thing shall be well
> By the purification of the motive
> In the ground of our beseeching.'

What does it feel like to pray? What seems to happen when we pray? What should happen? It is very difficult to answer these questions lucidly. Prayer is the most personal of all experiences; the stages of our growth in prayer vary so much with each individual; and our strivings have to be described in terms that easily lapse into metaphor for lack of exact words to describe intangible experience. I can only give an example of what may be experienced either in solitude or in the communal setting of a Friends' Meeting for worship:

First, we relax into a period of adjustment, opening the mind to what to us seems most purifying and true. There may then come a slow clarification of mind leading towards an inward realization of meaning and purpose, especially if we focus our thoughts on the person of Christ, who thus becomes our Mediator in the practice of prayer. Through Him, or through some words of His, we may gradually feel ourselves to be part of a Wholeness that imparts a sense of blessing and security. Through all this we are thinking; and yet not directing thought so much as allowing our thought to be directed. But to remain in this state of vague communication is not enough. Maybe, by conscious effort, we experience an outflow of the self to other selves — the subject 'I' becomes active — I love, I share, I accept, I will suffer. We thus pass from 'within' to 'without' and thus complete the full circle of prayer. The early vagueness takes on concreteness, a more precise and active form. We are thus projected into the realm of our neighbour; and in this realm we begin to think how we may serve him. Such a cycle of prayer may not be typical; it can have many variations and greatly different stresses in its different parts; it may take place in an entirely different sequence. What matters is that the complete prayer involves God, me, my neighbour.

In his diagnosis of prayer, William James insists that prayer must be *effective* if it is to prove itself more than mere illusion: 'If it be not effective, if it be not a give and take relation; if nothing be really transacted while it lasts; if the world is no whit different for its having taken place; then prayer, taken in this wide meaning of a sense that something is transacting, is, of course, a feeling of what is illusory.' I think William James is right. The test of the efficacy of prayer lies in its capacity to effect something. Now many people who would agree with James might agree for the wrong reasons. To take a crude example, they might petition God to satisfy some personal need, say a fur coat or a good job or a bicycle at Christmas; and if these desires were satisfied, by happy coincidence or by words whispered in the right ear, the petitioner might be led to believe that his prayer had been answered. But God is not interested in fur coats or bicycles. Such fringe needs do not come within the true range of prayer. They are irrelevancies to the essentials of life. Much more acceptable is the child's prayer, 'God bless mummy and daddy, and Jack and Jill, and please make me a good boy'. The effect here is to set the child's mind in the right direction, towards the 'neighbours', who are real persons in his little world. The 'set' in the fur-coat prayer is in the direction of securing things for ourselves. Petitionary prayer is quite natural but not as a means of 'extorting something from a grudging deity'. If we pray but discover that we have ceased to pray for others, we should realize that our supplications are perilously near the neurotic demands of the self-centred.

The effectiveness of prayer must be tested at a deeper level. Although it is not wrong to pray for health or success in our rightful concerns, for these are part of our lives which are God's concern also, we must bear in mind that what we desire most makes us what we are. Our desires are the raw material on which God works. In this way prayer becomes the training-ground of character. It is as a maker of personality that the *effect* of prayer must be judged. When we sincerely ask for guidance we are submitting our desires to God for his approval, and we shall usually find that no desire is quite the same when it has been honestly offered to God and returned to us for action. By training ourselves to accept the disciplines that come of purified desire we are adopting a practical but not a comfortable way of bringing ourselves into partnership with God. We shall also discover that no prayer has been fully prayed until it has initiated decision and constructive action. This, I think, is what William James means when he says there must be something 'really transacted'.

D.   IS PRAYER AUTO-SUGGESTION?

But is prayer merely auto-suggestion? Are we praying to ourselves after all? This is a question that must obviously arise in the mind of anyone who thinks, because, whatever the answer may be, there is no reason to believe that the normal psychological *mechanisms* of thinking and feeling should not operate during meditation and prayer.

Suggestion is a mental process involving the uncritical acceptance of ideas arising from external stimuli — from another person or from a book, for example. Auto-suggestion, or self-suggestion, is the same process, but in this case the idea accepted comes from the individual himself. Clearly there are parallels between the thinking-feeling states of a person who has accepted an idea under the conditions conducive to auto-suggestion and the thinking-feeling conditions of prayer. In both there is the initial need for relaxation and quiet which assist the effortless acceptance by the unconscious of the suggested idea. In both there is a concentration on the general result that is desired — in a sick person practising auto-suggestion, on the idea of health; in prayer it is concentration on the idea of God or on the active principle of Love. Prayer and auto-suggestion are in closest similarity during the state of meditation, when the whole person-ality seems to be quietly focused on a developing theme and is least conscious of outward interference. Prayer and auto-suggestion seem to differ most when prayer takes us outside ourselves to our neighbour, whereas auto-suggestion remains concentrated on self; although in each case our thought seems to be generated by the self. All these considerations suggest strong similarities between the psychology of prayer and auto-suggestion. If we accept this quite likely proposition, does this prove prayer to be merely auto-suggestion, a self-induced state of mental and emotional activity?

Our answer will depend entirely on whether we believe God exists. If we do not believe God exists then prayer is foolish; but auto-suggestion in some circumstances may be quite useful. We can 'auto-suggest' ourselves out of a state of fear, for instance. But we can also 'auto-suggest' ourselves into all kinds of illusion, whether harmless or harmful. In auto-suggestion the question of truth or untruth does not arise. But if our dominant idea in the prayer-state is that of a vital loving Person, it is to Him we surrender both our conscious and unconscious self, even if we do this through the normal psychological mechanism with which all men are endowed. As Streeter has remarked, 'it is the truth of the idea, not the mechanism of its acceptance, that makes it to be prayer . . . Prayer is a flight upwards, an offering of the mind to that which is more real than the self; auto-suggestion is a swoop downwards, a submission of the mind to an idea which is a creature of its own. Prayer brings the inspiration which comes of contact with a personality greater than our own; auto-suggestion in the last resort is of the nature of "dope" '. Moreover, if we believe God desires communication with His creatures, is it not reasonable to assume that He will use as the means of communica-tion the mental mechanism with which He has endowed us? Perhaps this idea is more easily acceptable by those who also believe that the God who is Beyond is also Within, and that it is only from within that we can know Him.

To believe that God exists removes the main obstacle to prayer by resolving the doubt that to pray is to delude oneself. Another obstacle is a sense of guilt. Nothing is so corroding and enervating as the depression that results from failure to live up to our own standards. Our conscience may be a good guide but, if too sensitive to our own shortcomings, may become a dangerous taskmaster. We may be sure that when we feel unable to pray our conscience is exacting too much of us. We must remember that God forgives the penitent sinner. The prodigal son was able to pray because he was sorry for his foolishness and because he was assured of his father's forgiveness. That is a healthy attitude to guilt. We have to confess our sins before God; and then we shall be able to forgive ourselves. It is most important to believe that it is right to forgive ourselves, for this self-forgiveness is the final release that enables us to *move on* in the process of building up our personality. We can make no progress if we are pursued constantly by a nagging sense of guilt which some dark and unwarranted interpretations of Christian belief seem to regard as the mark of a religious man. One of the notable characteristics of Fox's life is that, unlike so many religious reformers, he records no deep conviction of sin. It was not on an awareness of sin that he built his life but on the conviction of God's nearness and Christ's love.

There are so many aspects of prayer about which I have said nothing. My intention has largely been to examine its validity as the central religious activity, because doubt about prayer exercises the minds of so many people in an age where scepticism has become a primary virtue. Prayer like all religious experience has to be honestly tried before we can decide the truth of it for ourselves. I conclude, then, with the words of Thomas Kelly, who knew a great deal about it and who has more right than I have to speak intimately about the life lived in prayer:

'An inner, secret turning to God can be made fairly steady, after weeks and months and years of practice and lapses and failures and returns. . . . Begin now, as you read these words, as you sit in your chair, to offer your whole selves, utterly and in joyful abandon, in quiet, glad surrender to Him who is within. In secret ejaculations of praise, turn in humble wonder to the Light, faint though it be. Keep contact with the outer world of sense and meanings. Here is no discipline of absent-mindedness. Walk and talk and work and laugh with your friends. But behind the scenes keep up the life of simple prayer and inward worship. Keep it up throughout the day. Let inward prayer be your last act before you fall asleep and the first act when you awake. And in time you will find . . . "that those who have the gale of the Holy Spirit go forward even in sleep." '

Now we have discussed prayer we are ready to consider the Friends' manner of worship, for our worship is rooted in the prayers of our membership.

X

WORSHIP

'I myself, in part, am a true witness, who not by strength of argument, or by a particular disquisition of each doctrine, and convincement of my understanding thereby, came to receive and bear witness of the truth, but by being secretly reached by this life; for when I came into the silent assemblies of God's people, I felt a secret power among them, which touched my heart, and as I gave way to it, I found the evil weakening in me, and the good raised up.'

ROBERT BARCLAY

A. THE MANNER OF FRIENDS' WORSHIP

I REMEMBER well my first meeting for worship many years ago. At that time I knew little of Friends except through books. I had crept into the nearest meeting house to discover how this strange manner of worship really worked. I went in a mood of curiosity rather than in a reverent spirit; and therein lay my failure. What happened to me was certainly not comparable to Barclay's experience. I sat amidst a group of thirty or forty silent people, a mixed group of averagely intelligent and moderately prosperous-looking English citizens, and waited for something to happen — to happen not to me, but in the meeting. I found it most difficult to sit still. As the silence continued my body and mind were caught up in an increasing tension that became almost unbearable until I took myself in hand and deliberately relaxed. But still I waited, in a nervous expectancy, for someone to speak, for something to happen.

And then something quite startling did happen. A man rose to his feet and, with the fluency we tend to associate with the ranting preacher, spoke to his own home-made text 'Three per cent of salt', likening the Society of Friends to the salt that gives savour to the sea. But he had not proceeded far with his adulatory discourse before a white-haired woman rose to her feet and said in a clear firm voice, 'I hope our friend will sit down. We are

77

not gathered here to listen to the praises of the Society of Friends: we are here waiting upon God.' Our friend sat down with some protest, much discomforted. He too, it seemed, like me, was an intruder, but in his unfortunate case, an unsuitably vocal one. I had been present, I realized, on a rare occasion of 'eldering', when an Elder of the meeting had felt called upon to protect the worship of God from unworshipful sentiments. I later learned to know, love and admire this great woman Friend, Joan Mary Fry; but at that moment I only knew that her words had 'spoken to my condition'. I was at this meeting to wait upon God, and for no other purpose. I relaxed; and waited.

But waiting was very difficult because I did not know what I was waiting for, nor how to wait, nor how to focus my attention on an idea for more than a few minutes. Stray thoughts fluttered through my mind like butterflies finding no resting place. There was vocal ministry of an acceptable kind, but I have no memory of it. And yet I came away from that hour of very amateur silent worship with a dim awareness that here was an experience of some significance, too important to neglect lest there might be discovered one day, in the stillness, something rich and strange. Today, thirty-five years later, to miss my meeting for worship is a real deprivation. But this consummation has not been reached quickly or easily. For most of us waiting upon God in the stillness requires long practice, discipline, patience and much sincerity.

If we believe, as all Christians do, that God's spirit will break through into the human consciousness, then it is logical to believe that to wait for this to happen in the stillness is the most intimate form of divine communication with men. If God will speak to us, then we must prepare ourselves to listen. And Friends believe that the best form of corporate listening is a gathering of people who meet together in silence and in brotherhood. Thus the individual mystical relationship with God becomes part of a group mystical experience. Our sense of union with our Lord is bound up with our unity one with another. In many of his epistles, George Fox emphasises this dual rôle of true worship:

'All Friends mind that which is Eternal, which gathers your hearts together up to the Lord, and lets you see that ye are written in one another's Heart.'

It is this sharing of divine communication in group worship that has happily preserved Friends from an irresponsible reliance on individual infallibility. From long experience Friends have painfully come to realize that although a man may be in touch with God he is not thereby made free of all divine wisdom.

The only outward organization involved in a Friends' Meeting for worship is a place to meet in, be it meeting house, home or the open air; and an agreed time for meeting. Except for chairs or benches the meeting house is bare; there is no visible focus of interest, no altar, no pulpit. In the Catholic Church the altar is the focal point of worship; for the Protestant the pulpit; for the Society of Friends it is the inward experience of the individual within the communal experience of the gathered meeting. There is no beautiful liturgy framed in words of ancient and devout lineage, no music to blend mind with heart, no appeal to the senses, no communal hymn-singing to lift the voice in praise, no visible activity in the quiet expectancy. And yet is there not an aesthetic quality in stillness itself, something akin to the beauty of holiness that Jacob felt at Bethel? Is there not something more than a dull emptiness in the quiet faces that mask the rhythmic strivings of simple folk engaged upon the strenuous task of seeking the Beauty of Holiness Himself? As to activity, there is much of it in the poised concentration of the expectant mind as it seeks to be aligned with the will of the living God.

The manner of Friends' worship does indeed neglect much of what their fellow Christians believe to be intrinsically essential to the adoration of the Most High. Friends offer no criticism of what others deem necessary. Although in the more austere periods of Quaker history, when Friends felt they had a position to defend, music was wrongly regarded as an unseeming frivolity in a sober life, today Friends, in their homes and schools, give it a high place as one of the graces of living. Nevertheless, many would still feel that aesthetic sensibility is not basic to worship of God as they conceive such worship to be. When music and the visual arts are used to stimulate religious feeling the means, they would say, too easily becomes the focus of concern; the vehicle becomes confused with the end of the journey. The fruits of aesthetic appreciation are good; but they are not the same as the fruits of spiritual exercise.

One of the features of the Quaker way of worship that very soon appealed to me was the fact of its strongly social character. By 'social' I mean 'related to other persons'. It had been my experience in a variety of other churches, Catholic, Anglican and Free Church, that my attention travelled along a thread leading from me to the priest at the altar, or to the preacher in the pulpit, or may be to the organ and the choir, each in turn. But I have no memory of this binding thread passing from me *around* and *through* all those who are worshipping with me. There was far too much going on, far too much outwardly attracting my interest and even demanding my attention (e.g. timing my genuflections or finding my place in a book) to permit of a thought for my immediate neighbours. As a boy accustomed to a Friends' meeting once said to me after visiting the local church —'I had to stand up and do something just when I thought I was going to think.' But in a Quaker meeting I found that I was bound firmly to my fellow worshippers; they were the only visible distraction from my inward thoughts, apart from a passing cloud or a sparrow on a chimney pot if I gazed through a window of the meeting house. My fellow worshippers, known and un-known, were part of me and I of them; what I was trying to do they were trying to do. It was just God; and I and they. But they also represented all the world beyond the worshipping group, all other men, outside me. They were what I must be concerned about outwardly, as God was what I must be concerned about inwardly. And, and this is the crux, I knew I could not worship God adequately unless I imagined them in relation to God all the time. Thus, true worship takes on the rhythm of the pendulum — the swing outward follows the swing inward, each fortifying the other. The absence, then, of all distracting influences, whether of music, sermon or book, seemed to bring me nearer to the only two existences with which religion has anything to do. In the Friends' Meeting we are isolated with God and our neighbour.

B. THE METHOD OF FRIENDS' WORSHIP

There are good meetings and bad meetings, just as there are good sermons and bad sermons. But the indifferent sermon may find only one man at fault; the sterile meeting is everybody's fault, a result of shallow individual thinking and absence of group harmony. We are then constrained to ask with William Penn:

'When you come to your meetings . . . what do you do? Do you then gather bodily together only, and kindle a fire, compassing yourselves about with the sparks of your own kindling and so please yourselves . . . ? Or rather, do you sit down in True Silence, resting from your own Will and Workings, and waiting upon the Lord, with your minds fixed in the Light wherewith Christ has enlightened you, until the Lord breathes life in you, refreshes you, and prepares you, and your spirits and souls, to make you fit for his service . . . ?'

What do we do? Our answer to Penn's question will reveal something of the method and detail that go to make a fruitful Friends' Meeting. There are no doubt other answers, but this is how it appears to me. I shall not succeed in giving a complete picture because too many intangible factors are involved. Who has ever separated out the ingredients of an act of worship? Who, indeed, has ever worshipped perfectly, except perhaps for a brief moment?

Worship is primarily adoration. It is only through adoration that we can become more like what we adore. When this silent reverent adoration of God takes place our minds are lifted up, self retreats, and we find our love extending upwards to God and all about us to our friends. We become aware of God's activity in us and we find it both purifying us and directing our interest away from our selves to other selves.

By this pathetically vague and inadequate statement I am trying to say something quite definite; something that actually happens. We sit in the stillness, really loving, really caring for one another, slowly purging our minds of any tinge of bitterness, stilling criticism of any person worshipping with us. All irritations, all ungenerous thoughts must go; and they go most quickly when we try to imagine the perfect lovingness of the Source of love. We remember George Fox's advice not to look at evil, but to stay in the Light that reveals our frailty, and so pass evil by. That is the beginning of worship.

This worship is not 'based on silence' as Friends so often and so carelessly say, but on expectant waiting and striving. The silence is merely the condition in which we work — the water in which we swim, so to speak. It is not the silence that is active; it is we and God who are active. All the time we must remember that we are creating the conditions for God to speak to us. At the core of the Friends' Meeting lies a belief in the initiative of God. Only in this sense is the silence creative. Friends call such stillness both 'gathered' and 'covered'. Gathered because we rest in harmony with each other; covered because we know ourselves to be worshipping beneath the overshadowing wings of the loving and living God. Hence an active and vital meeting may well be a completely silent meeting. On the other hand a meeting too full of words can be a barren and unharmonious meeting; not gathered, because individuals have failed to establish their minds within the enfolding wings. I hope these similes of 'enfolding wings' and so on are not too vague to convey meaning. To me they are attempts to convey *felt* experience, and they seem to be the only way I can express such experience.

Meeting, then, is for worship, which begins in adoration of God, this adoration being the quickest means of eliminating the intrusion of the unworthy self. We need never worry about completely eliminating self. There must always be a subject as well as an object of any activity. By adoration we still the upsurges from that dark deep well of uncontrolled desires that so largely govern the lives of men. Their intrusion ruins worship by destroying the harmony of the meeting. But just because meeting is for worship, other good things follow. Because we have worshipped we have been guided and may be, but only may be, we have become instruments for guiding others. We have been strengthened, and, what is more, we have been straightened. Because we have loved each other we have taken the first step to loving all mankind.

There is a Quaker saying that we must come to meeting 'with hearts and minds prepared'; this is a way of saying that just as meeting should nourish our lives, so our lives should nourish our meeting. In effect, this implies that there is a place for brief acts of worship and prayer in the performance of our daily tasks throughout the week, so that we preserve continuing contact with the Life that becomes the primary influence in a meeting for worship. Thus the life of our solitariness, and the quality of our family life, become shared experience when we come together as a worshipping group. To be prepared for meeting does not mean that we should have a nice little sermon ready for the improvement of our friends on a Sunday morning.

It is well to remember that meeting begins when the first Friend has entered the meeting house. As each person enters he begins his worship in the stillness. Let not the murmur of voices in the lobby disturb us; it is best to regard minor disturbances as an opportunity for an exercise in concentration. When others join us they will know that the first worshippers are already engaged in 'driving away the shadows of self-will'. Pause for a moment as you read this and think of the wonder of this thing — that we join a group of people who are actively engaged in driving away the shadows of self-will! We sit down. Then we relax. We relax physically and emotionally, slowly releasing ourselves from the resentments and frustrations that clutter up our lives and separate us from our neighbours and from God. Thus we make ourselves at one with each other.

We shall not find this act of release come easily. Our minds will wander according to the state of our preparedness, with the rate at which the wheels of our own private little world are buzzing away. It is often useful to focus our thoughts on a person we know, to pray for a friend in need of comfort, or for a person we find it difficult to love. Or we may say deliberately with carefully chosen words a prayer of thanksgiving or praise, forming the words almost audibly, resisting the lazy tendency to be content with a vague uprising of undirected goodwill. Or we may concentrate on a word of Scripture, attempting to elucidate and develop its meaning. Nothing will help us more in our efforts to 'centre down' in this early period of worship than a few words of vocal prayer spoken reverently and quietly by one of the worshippers; nothing will more effectively deepen the quality of our silent thoughts and focus them where they will find some creative source of meditation.

We must not be worried if our efforts to concentrate on a fruitful theme meet with repeated defeat. We must feel encouraged in our early exercises if we have succeeded in holding a selfless

thought for only thirty seconds. Even the most secure and practised worshipper will often find his mind slipping away into
self-regarding irrelevance. Nor must we think that those still and
wise grey heads around us are concentrating solidly for the whole
hour. That seldom happens. For most of us there are periods,
short or long, of lucid contemplation when we feel that our small
light is strengthened by the Holy Spirit; there are periods, often
long, of arid wandering and vacancy.

It is clear, then, that the will has to play its part; but also the
intelligence and the imagination which are essential aids in assisting
the mind to separate out the relevant from the irrelevant. All the
time we are thinking; piecing together our own thoughts with
the vocal ministry, selecting and building into coherent wholes.
Then our vision widens and we go quietly along the path indicated
by a new insight, seeing applications of our hardly won truth
opening out before us.

I have spoken of the gathered silence and of an active and living
silence. There is also the *continuing* silence. Although we are all
enfolded in the stillness in unity of spirit, we may not all be
thinking the same thoughts. Our meditations will be partly
determined by the setting of our personal lives, which are all
different, by our personal strains and stresses, by our varied occupations, by our education and the peculiar set of our minds, by the
books we read, by our age and by our family preoccupations.
But if we are really *working* in worship, all these varied strands
of experience will be gradually tending in one direction —
towards God's word for us. Then, may be, like a white crested
wave, words will come out of the sea of silent worship to quicken
our imagination and sink back into the continuing flow of the
sea of prayer that gave them utterance. This is vocal ministry.

C. VOCAL MINISTRY

The spoken word in meeting must always arise as a natural and
inevitable outflow of the united continuing silence. Hence, when
we feel impelled to speak we must be as certain as we can be that
God speaks through us. We must 'have a sense of *being used*', says
Thomas Kelly, 'of being played upon, of being spoken through'.
When we decide that we have a message to give we must be

sure that we ought to give it, very sure that it has grown out of worship, very sure that we are not breaking clumsily, irreverently and irrelevantly, into a strain of thought already established. This certainty we shall not have if we come to meeting as individuals with a personal axe to grind, and remain as isolated individuals throughout the meeting, tense with personal concerns, neglectful of the loving fellowship around us, and with an unexamined point of view we are determined to express.

Vocal prayer and vocal ministry in a Friends' Meeting may be likened to a many faceted jewel, each face reflecting light from the whole. Or again, they may be regarded as a progressive building up of truth, as a series of bricks laid one upon another as in the rising courses of a good building. But how often do we see a heap of stones! Vocal ministry should be *responsible*; that is to say, responsive to the direction other words have taken, and subjected to close scrutiny before spoken. It should be *reconciling*; healing not destructive, harmonizing, not argumentative. There is no place for debate in a meeting for worship. It should be *simple*, free from repetition; it should be brief rather than long; restrained in manner. Oratory is not indicated. And it should be *sincere*. A few stumbling sentences spoken from the heart and growing out of deeply felt experience are worth all the eloquence in the world. The fatal fluency of the verbal type is not an asset to Friends' Meetings.

The listening group should be very tender to those who have spoken, remembering that to many the spoken word does not come easily, although it may be the outcome of much prayer and exercise of spirit. We should be tender, sensitive, in two ways: First we must not be over critical of ministry that to sophisticated minds sets forth an unacceptable morality or theology. Humbly acknowledging our own inadequacy, we must seek to see and preserve the element of truth in what we hear. God will take care of the untruth. Secondly, we must above all refrain from crashing into the silence following a piece of vocal ministry, and crash is not too strong a word, with a message of our own, before the listening worshippers have had time to ponder the words they have just heard. To do so really breaks the continuing silence; thought ceases to ripen; and we may have to begin our meeting over again.

We have to be so sensitive and generous with regard to vocal ministry; so humble and so restrained. If we feel impelled to speak it is far better to say too little than too much; far better that another Friend should complete or continue our theme than that we should complete it ourselves. How often must we humbly acknowledge the greater aptness and power of the following speaker's contribution to the theme we may have initiated. And with what wonder and with what joy may we rest thankful that we resisted the less urgent promptings to rise to our feet when another Friend says so much better what we had intended to say. How good are the words of Thomas Kelly when he says: 'No jealousy, no regrets that *he* didn't think of saying that, but only gratitude that the angel has come and troubled the waters and that many are finding healing through the one Life. A gathered meeting is no place for the enhancement of private reputations, but for self-effacing pliancy and obedience to the whispers of the Leader.'

Vocal ministry is not to be confined to the learned or vocal or the experienced or aged or dyed-in-the-wool Quaker. And God speaks equally to men and women. From the simple devout mind, from the busy housewife, from the farmer close to the soil, from the craftsman working on tough material among tough men, so often comes the deeply felt message of consolation or challenge that sets the direction for a perfect meeting for worship. The Light shines through all.

The last few minutes of worship are very precious. At the end of a good meeting we are truly gathered; silence is the only medium for our closing thoughts. Only under the most impelling sense of urgency, critically examined, should the stillness be broken. We should cultivate a sensitive responsibility for these last few minutes, for it is quite out of the spirit of true worship for a Friend to rise in vocal ministry and disturb the sense of completion that the close of worship demands. Only a few words of prayer can possibly be appropriate at this point. We are released and refreshed if we have truly worshipped, if we have been prayerful, responsible, restrained and sincere.

XI

A CREEDLESS FAITH

*'This is to inform you that all our works and declarations . . . do
clearly testify . . . that God who is the only wise, omnipotent, and
everlasting God we do own and believe in, who is creator of all things
both in heaven and earth . . . and that Jesus Christ is his beloved and
only begotten son . . . who was conceived by the Holy Ghost . . . and
we do believe that he is alone redeemer and saviour . . . who saves us
from sin . . . and was crucified for us in the flesh without the gates of
Jerusalem, and that he was buried and rose again on the third day . . .
that there is no other foundation to be laid but what is laid, even
Christ Jesus.'*

GEORGE FOX
(*Letter to Governor of Barbados*, 1671)

THIS BRIEF EXTRACT from a long declaration of faith written in
defence of the little group of Quakers in Barbados, on a particular
occasion of difficulty, has sometimes been an embarrassment to
modern Friends as it contains almost the whole of the Apostle's
Creed, either word for word or in close paraphrase. No good
churchman could quarrel with any of this most orthodox confession of the founder of Quakerism, with its clear indication that
early Friends did not deny orthodox Christian beliefs; in fact,
they took them for granted. Their criticism was directed at the
interpretation and use of the creeds as tests of Christian faith, not
at the beliefs themselves. As with the Scriptures, Fox appealed
away from credal definitions of the fourth century to the experience of primitive Christians and to the events that inspired this
experience. We shall miss the essence of the Quaker protest if we
fail to realize that Fox was entirely concerned to emphasize old
and forgotten aspects of the Christian gospel, not to preach a new
gospel of his own.

Hence when early Friends were asked whether they accepted
the definitions of Christian doctrine formulated by medieval
church councils they protested that they were being asked the

87

wrong question. The new insights, gained by their vivid experience of the 'break through' of the Holy Spirit into their own lives, impelled them to ask if the Christ of the creeds was alive in men's souls *now*, whether he was their redeemer *now*, whether he was resurrected in their hearts *now*. It was not definitions of belief that were important but living in the spirit of the creed. For are not credal definitions by their nature second-hand, a discovery of a past age, very important, but, as Harold Loukes has said, 'a statement in the past tense?' We are faced again with Fox's challenge: 'You will say, Christ saith this, and the apostles say this, but what canst *thou* say?' These were the reasons why early Friends refused to regard subscription to a precise definition of belief as a test of Christian faith.

But, as Friends' views on the creeds have developed, another consideration has entered into their refusal to be bound by definition. It is the view that truth is an everlastingly unfolding phenomenon, that God continues to reveal himself to men, and that from the foundation-truths of Christ's life, death and resurrection, new wonders are still to come. One of the dangers of formulated statements of belief, as *Christian Faith and Practice*, our Quaker 'Book of Discipline', explains, is that they tend to 'crystallize thought on matters that will always be beyond any final embodiment in human language'. On this matter Rufus Jones has best expressed the modern Quaker position: 'the essential nature of man's being and his immortal destiny, the true reality and character of God and His relation to human history, the tragic fact of sin and the way of salvation, the truth of inspiration of Scripture and the Gospel revelation of Christ, will always concern serious men and women. But those questions cannot be answered once for all in magic phrases, nor by fulminations of historic councils and assemblies. They are as profound as life itself and they must be re-thought and re-expressed through the growing experience of the race. Strict intellectual agreement on these great issues of the mind can hardly be expected or desired, nor should matters which involve the *unfinished pursuit of truth* form the essential basis of church membership'.

Thus the Quaker protest against creeds was not against the beliefs formulated but against the danger of their formulation in words, no matter how logical and consistent, that would render these beliefs incapable of expansion as personal experience of the Holy Spirit enriched their meaning. We believe that the Church would have been saved much bitter controversy and that it would have avoided the clash with scientific views of the universe that so seriously damaged the Christian message in the nineteenth century, if it had not been restricted by its own credal statements. Nevertheless Friends should take to heart Von Hügel's criticism that they have been 'historically ungrateful' to the Church's testimony of Christian fundamentals throughout the ages. Where would Fox have been, and where would Christianity be, if the Church had neglected to codify its teaching into a body of conviction that resisted the assaults of fantastic heresies and the corroding influence of sentimental vagueness. I have often confessed to a somewhat guilty thankfulness that Quakerism did not appear before the great medieval cathedrals had been built to the glory of God; and in a similar way Friends should be grateful to the Church for maintaining the great truths of which they became the heirs.

Even though Friends reject the use of a formal confession of faith the creeds remain to challenge them to think through their own position. Meditation on the Apostles' Creed should impel us to discover for ourselves what we do believe, which is a religious and intellectual exercise no Christian can risk neglecting. For belief determines attitude and action. What we believe, we are; what we do, we believe. When we ponder, item by item, on the statements in this central creed of the church, we find, as Job did in a similar situation, that we are faced with wonders and mysteries that defy a purely rational response but which, nevertheless, leave us restless until a combined operation of intelligence and imagination leads us in the direction in which an answer may be found. We respond partly with affirmative conviction, partly with doubt, sometimes with denial; here we accept with faith because we want some belief to be true, and there we reject because we fear what may be true.

When I confront myself with the Apostles' Creed I find that I can accept more of its affirmations than I could have done if I had subjected myself to this scrutiny when I first joined the Society of Friends.

Do I believe in *God the Father Almighty, maker of heaven and earth*? Yes I do. But 'heaven' I assume to be the expanding universe of which the earth is but a single planet among billions. I believe that this universe has evolved and is evolving under law, the *logos*, its physical nature progressively explained by the scientist, its spiritual counterpart by Christ and his saints. I believe also that there is much yet to be revealed to man both in the physical and spiritual realms; and I do not expect scientific revelations to disturb my belief in a spiritual realm over which God reigns.

Do I believe in *Jesus Christ his only Son our Lord*? I believe in the historical Jesus, that His life on earth was subject to the conditions of time and place and to the physical limitations of human kind. I believe also that in Him the divine meets the human by God's initiative in 'breaking through' into the consciousness of men; and that Jesus Christ is the only Son because He alone perfectly expresses the full nature of God. I accept the statement that He was *conceived by the Holy Ghost* as a declaration of the inflowing of the Holy Spirit in absolute degree into a human soul. I do not believe that Jesus *was born of the Virgin Mary*; I do not find this helpful or necessary, because belief in miraculous conception and birth seems to deny the full humanity of Jesus, separates Him from suffering mankind and renders less meaningful the quality of His own suffering. At no point in the Gospels does He claim miraculous birth and His divine power and quality is too obvious in His works to require the support of a myth common the world over to many pagan religions.

That Jesus *suffered under Pontius Pilate, was crucified, dead and buried*, is a historical fact of supreme significance, for here divine Love challenges the massed power of organized worldliness, not with an argument, but with the fact of sacrificial and redemptive suffering. The Cross turns our values topsy-turvy. In the ideally wrong death of the ideally good man we are confronted in one dramatic hour with the *quality* of Creative Life. The situation defies intellectual analysis; and it is not in theology that we shall find its meaning. Its significance can be apprehended only by a supreme effort of the imagination and a denial of common sense. That is why the simple can believe more easily than the logician. In presenting suffering as redemptive the Cross declares man to be God's responsibility to the uttermost extent of divine Love.

Thus Christ gives dignity to the human race. Men are worth dying for. When we wish to get clear about the nature of Reality, that is, about those aspects of the universe that we must regard as facts, we can no more pass by the death of Christ than we can defy the law of gravity. Jesus died to save men. This is one of the articles of Christian faith that I have always found difficulty in believing because I fear the responsibilities involved. But I am reminded of William Temple's question: Which is it better to be, 'the man who finds it difficult to believe that Christianity is true but hopes that it is; or the man who believes that it is true but wishes it wasn't?'

While accepting in this faulty way the foundation statements of the creeds I would not wish to make them a test of my right to belong to a branch of the Christian Church. Is it not better for many of us to use our most imaginative perceptions to realize that God has revealed Himself not only in the wonders of the physical universe but in the wonder of a human life. This glimpse of what God is like impels us to trust what Jesus said and did, and also what he said he was —'I and the Father are one.' To trust is not to be completely certain; it is to go forward, not outwardly armed with a creed, but inwardly determined to 'get to know that we know these realities by finding our knowledge approving itself to us as fruitful, in a thoroughly living and practical, in a concrete, not abstract, not foretellable, in a quite inexhaustible way'.

XII

THE SACRAMENTAL LIFE

'If I then, the Lord and Master, have washed your feet, ye also ought to wash one another's feet. For I have given you an example, that ye also should do as I have done to you.'

ST JOHN XIII, 14-15

'The truth must eat out the ceremony, and the substance the sign; the more the baptism of Christ comes in, the more the baptism with water will go out.'

WILLIAM DELL

APART, PERHAPS, from their form of corporate worship nothing more distinguishes Friends from the main body of their Christian brethren than their neglect of the sacrament of Holy Communion. In rejecting this central and most beautiful of all the Church's liturgical offices, Friends have been guided by their desire to place no reliance on a ritual act that claims a uniquely sacred efficacy. Again the emphasis is laid not on the symbol but on its underlying reality, not on the eating of the bread or on the drinking of the wine, but on the inward flowing of the divine Will expressed outwardly in a life in which love renders every act a sacrament, a holy thing. Believing, as indeed most Christians do, that what matters most is the taking of the Christ-life into our own frail personality, that we inwardly experience its energizing power in every thought and in every human encounter, Friends have consistently turned away from ritual practices that use material aids to spiritual understanding. Nevertheless, they have always striven to remain faithful to the spiritual realities for which the sacraments stand. These differences of method in worship are no doubt a matter of temperament and upbringing. Friends believe that they come to know these same realities as vividly and as rewardingly in their silent meetings for worship.

It may be argued that in thus relinquishing this most cherished

and long established means of bringing the believer into communion with his Lord, Friends are neglecting Christ's own
command that his followers should 'do this in remembrance of
me'. The answers Friends give to this accusation are based partly
on their early experience and partly on a different interpretation
of Christ's injunction.

In Fox's day, and for many centuries before his time, the
manner and meaning of the Holy Communion had engendered
some of the bitterest controversies and divisions in Christian
history. Early Friends were not favourably impressed with a
practice that seemed to them to encourage neither holiness nor
true communion between Christians. To them a simple act of
fellowship, for surely this is what the Last Supper was, seemed to
have degenerated into a sacerdotal exclusiveness rather than a
reverent use of symbols 'to sanctify the whole material life and
make it transparently radiant with the spiritual'. Having discovered a deep harmony and fellowship in a loving act of silent worship,
the baptism of the spirit became to them more vital than baptism
by water; and the communion of the soul directly with the
'Presence in the midst' more efficacious than the symbolic communion wrought out of bread and wine and the offices of a
priest. They feared to resort to a practice, no matter how reverently conducted, in which lurked the danger of substituting a
form of words associated with material food for first-hand
experience 'in the life'. They shrank from entering upon a complex
situation where symbol and reality were not clearly defined, in
which the symbol, intended to concentrate the mind of the
worshipper on the gift of grace, might well obscure the end which
it exists to serve.

Modern Friends find this early intuitive objection to the
Eucharist ceremony supported by the doubts of some modern
scholars concerning the historical validity of the claim that it was
actually instituted by Jesus. In support of this view, which is
sanctioned by other scholars, but by no means all, we may
mention two names well-known in English biblical scholarship.
Hastings Rashdall in his *Bampton Lectures*, says that the words in
Luke xxii, 'this do in remembrance of me', are a late addition to
the text, and declares that there is nothing to suggest that our
Lord had the intention of founding a permanent rite of any kind.

Again, in his *Conflict of Religions in the Early Roman Empire*, T. R. Glover declares that 'Jesus instituted no sacraments'. In view of these opinions of biblical scholars Friends cannot be accused of lightly rejecting a command of Jesus for which there seems to exist only slender evidence.

There is, of course, no doubt that the celebration of the Last Supper formed part of the worship of the early Church, but it seems clear that this rite was a later, although quite early, development from the 'love feast' of the little groups of Christians who gathered together in a community meal in memory of their Lord, an occasion on which they were especially aware of the Presence in their midst. It was from this simple 'communion' of the faithful that gradually developed a rite of mysterious and even magical import, dependent on priestly mediation, from which those who participated were deemed to receive a miraculous gift of grace withholden from those who had not partaken in the mystery. There is something here so closely parallel to the practices of the mystery religions of the Roman Empire that one cannot forbear suggesting that the Church found it necessary to adopt a compensating practice of its own.

But even if the institution of the Lord's Supper had been more clearly evident in the synoptic Gospels it is doubtful whether Friends would have changed their views. Their guide was the Gospel of St John in which they found the sacrament of life symbolized by service, and the expression of communion an entirely spiritual experience of the living Spirit of Christ. 'I am the bread of life': the bread Jesus offered to His inquiring disciples was the bread of God '*that cometh down from heaven* and giveth life unto the world'. This discourse in the sixth chapter can even be read as a declaration of Jesus that the bread of the communion is not the material bread that plays its part in the Eucharist ceremony:

'He who feeds on my flesh and drinks my blood possesses eternal life . . . for my flesh is real flesh and my blood is real drink. He who feeds on my flesh and drinks my blood remains within me, as I remain within him. . . . Such is the bread which has come down from heaven:'

The following words suggest that Jesus draws a clear contrast between the 'real food' and the ordinary bread which men eat:

'Your ancestors ate their bread and died, but he who feeds on this bread will live for ever.'

(Moffat Version)

What matters is the inward acceptance of the Christ Spirit, not the physical eating of material bread, even if this bread symbolizes everlasting realities.

But it was no reference to particular texts that impelled Friends to emphasize the purely spiritual nature of communion. No doubt they found in the New Testament generally and in St John in particular what they were looking for, which was an interpretation of religion in terms of a spiritual life that proved its quality in a moral life. Friends still regard the story of the Last Supper as described in the Fourth Gospel as the true sacrament of life. Here the central act is not the breaking of bread but the washing of the disciple's feet. In this symbolism we see Jesus' own declaration of his purpose as recorded in Mark (x, 45):

'For the Son of Man himself has not come to be served but to serve and to give his life a ransom for many.'

The washing of the feet and the Cross are one. The divine humility, which is the spirit in which love is expressed, is demonstrated during this precious evening meal in the lowliest act of service the slave performs for his master; likewise, on the day of agony that is soon to come Jesus knows that the supreme service of love has yet to be performed. William Temple in *Readings in St. John's Gospel* points out the dual significance of the washing of the feet. He says that man's humility does not begin with the giving of service but with the readiness to receive it, to receive it from men and from God: whether in small things or great, in the washing of feet or in the service of the Cross. When men are capable of receiving the loving service of others they are fit to serve others in God's way. This way is service in fellowship and service through suffering.

I am aware that some commentators regard the washing of

feet as a symbol of the Christian sacraments of Baptism and the Eucharist and not 'a detached action containing in itself a merely ethical lesson'. If we presuppose the earlier institution of the Eucharist ceremony such a view is obviously tenable, but is this not reading more into the situation than is warranted? We are faced with the simple statement 'I have given you an example that ye also should do as I have done to you.' This is a truly ethical injunction, given in a setting from which develops the supreme commandment — that ye love one another: 'By this shall all men know that ye are my disciples, if ye have love one to another.' Surely in this saying and in this demonstration of the way love is manifested, by loving *service*, Jesus is telling His friends that the proof of love within the heart is its outward exercise in the hands that wash the feet. Jesus shows the fruits of eating 'the bread which has come down from heaven', making quite clear to His disciples that these fruits of the 'real food' do not consist in a comforting sense of special privilege, but in the humble duty of serving men in the hard world in which He is soon to leave them. The spiritual life and the moral life are one. It is just this that Friends call the sacramental life, the life in which every humble act of love is as significant as any ritual act on a special church occasion. And the emphasis is laid on the quality of life that naturally issues in a *continuing* sacrament in which the Real Presence is continuingly felt to be quietly, unobtrusively, but in very truth, guiding the whole personality into a loving relationship with other personalities.

In a similar way Friends have sought for a baptism of the spirit rather than baptism by water as a sign of their entry into the Christian fold. The Nicodemus passage in the third chapter of St John's Gospel is read not as indicating the requirement of water baptism but as declaring the need for spiritual rebirth. Jesus does, indeed, relate the two types of baptism, for baptism by water was an ancient Jewish rite with which he had no quarrel, and when the Evangelist wrote these words it had become the practice of the young church to use this rite as a visible sign of entry into the community of Christians. Nevertheless, a reading of the passage leaves little doubt that entry into the Kingdom of God was possible only to those who experience the cleansing power of the Holy Spirit to a degree that reverses the whole trend of their worldly life. It was this baptism of the Spirit that is well-defined as being 'born anew'; for the 'old Adam' dies and the new man is born. Here again emphasis on the efficacy of the material symbol encounters the danger that the baptized Christian may assume all to be well; that he will think salvation *has* come from the magical efficacy of the holy water, rather than that it *will* come from 'a clear life ensuing'.

For these reasons, then, Friends have relinquished the outward sacraments, not finding them 'necessary to salvation'. Some today who have joined the Society of Friends from other branches of the Christian community have not found it easy to deny themselves participation in the Lord's Supper, having found in truth that the outward and visible sign helps them to receive the inward spiritual grace. We recognize humbly that this is indeed one of the ways in which the Christian can come nearer to his Lord. The manner of receiving the Holy Spirit matters little when in very deed He comes, His grace to impart. But Friends remain convinced that 'the more the baptism of Christ comes in, the more the baptism with water will go out'.

XIII

SIN AND SUFFERING

For whether they looked upward they saw
the Divine Vision,
Or whether they looked downward they still
saw the Divine Vision,
Surrounding them on all sides beyond sin
and death and hell.

WILLIAM BLAKE

'I will arise and go to my father, and will say unto him, Father, I have
sinned against heaven, and before thee, and am no more worthy to be
called thy son.'

LUKE XV, 18-19

ALTHOUGH FRIENDS have suffered much for conscience sake and still call their executive committee the Meeting for Sufferings, a reminder of its original purpose, there is very little in Quaker literature that squarely faces the problem of suffering. Search the index of any book on Quakerism and it is unlikely that any reference to the problem of evil and pain will be found there. There is no mention of the problem *as a problem* in the quite voluminous *Christian Faith and Practice*, which outlines the spiritual experiences of the Society of Friends during three hundred years. This strange omission may be partly due to the fact that Quakerism has produced few theologians. Another reason is that Friends have always been more concerned with dealing with the evil they have found in themselves and in the world than in seeking to explain why it is there. In this way they have shown practical sense but have paid too little attention to the fact that the existence of evil is a potent generator of doubt concerning the existence of God.

Briefly, the problem is this: If God created all things, if God is good and loving, how is it that pain and sin so continuously afflict His creatures? Are we to accept the apparent contradiction that a good God is responsible for the evil that abounds in every corner of His creation? The answer to this question is much more readily given by the atheist than by the Christian. For the atheist God does not exist; we are a material part of a physical universe in which nature, 'red in tooth and claw', takes its toll in a purposeless evolutionary process. The atheist, then, solves the problem by saying that it does not exist. But tied up with the problem of evil is the problem of good. Evil cannot exist without good; we can only say a thing is evil when it is placed in contrast with its opposite. There is, then, a 'problem of good' to be dealt with as well as a problem of evil. And here the atheist is not so well placed as the Christian. How does the atheist account for the existence of good? Do the blind forces of the evolutionary process throw up by accident the sublime sacrificial qualities we see in the saintly leaders of the human race? Can we account for Socrates, Jesus and Gandhi by the atheist's line of argument?

The Christian answer to the problem of both good and evil is not an explanation at all; it is rather an acceptance of a challenge that requires us to decide where we stand — on the side of good, on the side of evil, or on the fence. In other words, we are not asked to argue, but to discover truth in the travail of experience. Before we elaborate a little on the nature of this challenge it is important to sort out the different categories of suffering which afflict mankind. Pain and evil are not the same things although they are part of the same problem because so much pain is the result of the criminal wickedness of irresponsible men.

A very large area of physical pain is protective, merely part of the warning apparatus of our delicate nervous system without which many of us would be limbless and deformed. A good deal of mental pain results from failure to face life in the right way; the same may be said of many diseases which result from foolish living. These beneficent categories of pain are not part of our problem. Even pain suffered because of the foolishness of others may well be dismissed as remediable if there is a chance of reducing the total sum of stupidity among those who cause pain.

But even if we can accept our afflictions thus far, we may reasonably protest that there is far more pain in the world than can be accounted for by human folly, or that can be willingly accepted as a chastening discipline for our moral welfare. There is a tragic immensity of wholly innocent suffering that remains without explanation or justification on any human criterion of justice. We are faced with the devastation of flood and earthquake, in which insensate nature claims her victims in the animate world. But even this passionless infliction of suffering puzzles us less than the man-inflicted agonies of mind and body that result from the criminal wickedness of wars and other forms of human conflict. It is the suffering of the innocent that most stimulates our doubt in the beneficence of our Creator. Better believe in no God at all than pin our faith to an eternal Fool who destroys the finest product of his creation.

We remain perplexed; but also with this thought: that a world in which the innocent never suffered from the wickedness of others, in which every man received the penalties he deserved, might be a 'just' world, but it would be a world where human responsibility for others counted for nought. We shall not find the explanation on the level of justice. To seek it on this level is to face defeat, for justice is not the supreme good. Christian doctrine offers a way out beyond justice, pointing not to the solution of a mystery but to the painful conquest of the inevitable. Nothing in the Gospels explains pain or evil; Christ showed us how to meet the challenge. And that is all. Briefly, then, we may say that the problem of pain and evil can be solved up to a point but that from this point there remains only a challenge, which we face with an act of faith and will, or refuse to face.

We begin by accepting the self-evident proposition that evil could not exist without good. We can just imagine a world where only good existed; it would be a queer world, free from struggle and rather uninteresting. But we cannot imagine a world where only evil existed because evil is only evil when it is in conflict with its opposite. If there were no goodness there would be no sin. The second proposition we must accept is that goodness is a moral concept bound up with human relationships. What is good binds men together; what is evil separates and destroys them. Love is good because it binds men in a reciprocal relationship of service; hatred, the opposite of love, is what destroys this fellowship. We can put this in another way: goodness is love extended beyond the bounds of self; sin is desire directed to our own self at the expense of others. We become sinners when we build up a false-self which feeds on *my* and *mine* and separates the self from *thy* and *thine*. In this way men become separated from God because it is only through men that we can love God. Again, we remember —'For their sakes I sanctify myself.' In thus refusing the fellowship of men we might almost say that men themselves create evil. And from this human source of evil, in which self becomes our god, there extend in ever-widening circles nearly all the avoidable evils that afflict the innocent — cruelties, injustices, the lusts for power and possessions, the ravages of war, and such outrages on mankind as the homeless refugee who starves in a world of plenty. The point need not be stressed for a generation that has tasted so freely of the poisonous fruit of misdirected desire.

There is only one Christian explanation of man's deliberate choice of evil rather than of good, and only one valid accusation we can level against God in regard to it. This explanation is to be found in the Christian doctrine of free-will. As biological beings we are creatures of impulse, as children of God we are gifted with the power of using our instinctive nature to carry us onward into a realm of living where appetite is governed by the sovereignty of spirit. Our animal heritage becomes evil when not so used. Evil appears when the divinely created will turns away from its divine origin and seeks its own separate satisfaction. Thus evil is a perversion, a disharmony in the personality. And God took the risk of leaving men free to choose between the creative and destructive, between good and evil.

'See, I have set before thee this day life and good, and death and evil.'

In so doing God elevated the dignity of man, made life far more difficult but infinitely more worth living, and also made it possible for man to be devil or saint, or something of both. Only for giving us this dangerous freedom can we criticize God.

Thus man becomes free to worship his divine Creator or himself, and a good part of the evil in the world has followed from man's choice of the second alternative. Sin is involved when we see the better and follow the worse. The Christian doctrine of free-will, then, does something to explain the presence of evil, but there remains no conceivable justification for a large area of pain, especially that inflicted by killing or deforming diseases, where seemingly meaningless suffering destroys the beauty of childhood or cuts short the beneficence of good lives. This is inexplicable. And there is nothing to be done about the inexplicable but to face it without repining; to face it with the determination that if the dreaded ill should choose us for its host we shall strive to meet it with the courage and imagination that the inexplicable always demands.

This attitude is so fundamental to the acceptance of certain forms of suffering that I must break through the intimacy of a deep family sorrow to explain what I mean. . . . The moment of revelation came to me just two months before the death of a very dear companion, whose active life had been a model of creative and selfless service. For many months she had fought tenaciously against the remorseless strokes of a rare and inevitably fatal disease, an affliction that seemed so senseless, so wasteful of a noble spirit, as to evoke all human doubts about a beneficent providence. In a weak moment I remarked to her, 'Isn't it strange that this should have happened to us?' She looked at me in surprise and said, 'But if it happens, why shouldn't it happen to us?'

For the first time in my life the full meaning of the Cross was given to me. I found myself confronted with that finest essence of the imagination which unselfconsciously and willingly shares pain with all mankind. I saw the Cross, the Cross of Jesus and the cross of humanity, as the final service of love, pain as the final sharing of love, the final argument that has no roots in logic, carrying its winged appeal beyond all reason and philosophy. I saw here the humble human person sharing in the pain of mankind and in the divine pain and sacrifice that Christ shares with us. And I realized that there are some ways of dealing with pain that transform the sufferer into a socially creative person. Thus we are left with no resentment, only with a deep thankfulness that flows over grief and deprivation, all self-pity and regret obliterated by the final victory. We may grieve at the sinfulness of men that made the Cross inevitable; but we rejoice and stand amazed with gratitude before the vision of Love thus fully and finally expressed.

Thus the Christian answer to the problem of pain comes not

by the way of logic but by the way of a certain kind of response
to an accepted fact. The same is true of the Christian way with
evil. The true Christian attitude to evil has been overlaid by
unwarranted assumptions derived from the Genesis myth of the
Fall of Man. The Old Testament myth represents an early attempt
to explain man's proclivity to sin; but there is no emphasis on
this explanation in any other part of the Bible. There is only one
other reference to the Fall in the whole of the Old Testament, and
only an oblique reference by St Paul in the New. From the teaching of Jesus it is completely absent. There is no place in His
Gospel for the idea of man's total depravity, because He did not
regard men as totally lost to the influence of the Good. In every
contact He made with a human soul He spoke to the Light that
He knew was there. The Christ who declared that the Kingdom
of God is within had no lot with those who so debased the temple
of the Holy Spirit. The real source of the idea of total depravity
is St Augustine who burdened the Church with this gloomy
doctrine from the fourth century onwards. It was not derived
from either Jesus or His apostle Paul.

In his attitude towards the struggle of the Christian with the evil
that is in him George Fox is much nearer to his Master than those
who look too fearfully at sin in their effort to overcome it.

'The Lord doth show unto man his thoughts, and discovereth
all the secret workings in man. A man may be brought to see
his evil thoughts and running mind and vain imaginations,
and strive to keep them down, and to keep his mind in, but
cannot overcome them nor keep his mind within to the Lord.
Now in this state and condition submit to the spirit of the
Lord, that shows them, and *he that has discovered them will
destroy them.*'

The emphasis here, as in all the writings of early Friends, is
not on the evil that has to be overcome but on the Light of Christ
that discovers it. Keep 'on top' of sin and confusion, concentrate
on the upward purpose, mind and observe 'that in us which
turns against sin and darkness', and sin will wither away for lack
of nourishment. Seek ye first the Kingdom of God; pursue the
good and leave the evil to God.

But there is more than this to be said about sin in the Christian theme, for lying at the core of Christian doctrine is the belief that Christ, once and for all, by his death made possible our salvation from the results of our sins. Here we find ourselves in the midst of the problem of the Atonement. Put in the simplest terms the question is: What difference has the death of Christ made in man's relation to God, especially regarding God's forgiveness of our sins? This question of the Atonement — how it works, was it necessary, ought we to bother about it? — is a source of bewilderment for many sincere believers. We are easily willing to concede that Christ's life and the manner of His death had made a difference to men and women ever since. It is part of Christian doctrine that Christ's sacrifice did something for the salvation of men. But the several theories as to *how* He did something are not part of Christian doctrine; they represent attempts of theologians to explain the mystery, among which we can take our choice. And some of these theories, whose origins take us back into Jewish and early Christian history, are not very attractive.

There are two groups of theories, the *subjective* and the *objective*. In the subjective or moral theory Christ's death saves by its profoundly moving power, so revealing the infinity of God's forgiveness and of His love for men that their minds are stirred to repentance by the contemplation of it, and are thus turned (converted) to a new way of life. The essence of the objective theories is that on Calvary Christ not only did something for men but that He also did something to God. Briefly, God forgives because Christ died. It is worth while to dwell for a moment on the two ancient theories that present Christ's death as a ritual sacrifice, the one to the Devil, the other to God, because these have still their ancient appeal to crude belief and their corresponding appeal to ridicule. First, there is the view that by His death Christ won for God the final victory over the forces of evil and thus destroyed for ever the devil's dominion over men. Secondly there is the 'ransom' theory — that because God demands punishment for sin before forgiveness is possible Christ bore the penalty on our behalf, and thus made it possible for God to forgive us. There is also another sacrificial theory, still popular in the revivalist world, that Christ freely offered His life as a sacrifice which thereafter becomes the cleansing power for sin-stained souls. (We remember the oft-used phrase 'washed in the blood of the Lamb'.)

I have dwelt on these theories of the Atonement because they are still obstacles to a reasonable faith. The cruder objective theories, steeped as they are in primitive ritual, I find quite untenable and utterly inconsistent with the God of justice and love whom Christ portrayed. A God who was willing to accept the suffering of the innocent in propitiation for the sins of the guilty is no God for me. We may well ask with John Oman, 'can we honestly believe that God would be satisfied with anything so unreal and perverted; or could we with any honesty avail ourselves of it if He were?' As to Christ's conquest of the devil, a personality concerning whose existence there are now doubts, we may say that He did indeed rise in victory over the dark forces in the hearts of His contemporaries that brought Him to His death. But every man who contemplates Christ's victory knows full well that sin is not conquered in his own heart. We remain sinners. Was Christ's victory, then, not a final conquest, but rather a demonstration of a method, the only method, by which victory can be won, and must be won, over and over again as long as life flows in us?

Christ did not die to change God's mind; he died to reveal it. He did not try to save us by 'the threat of hell or the bribe of heaven'. He died to save us from our sins by opening before us another world, as real and as present as the world in which we live our physical lives. On the Cross we witness Him in this world; we see Him accepting its standards and exercising its power. And we find it to be a world where love supplants legality, and, inevitably, therefore, where forgiveness follows from love — 'Father, forgive them, for they know not what they do.' There is nothing here about ransom or substitution or justice; only an agonized invitation to become members with Him of an entirely real and effective new order in which to live is to be changed, purged, forgiven, re-created. The forgiveness of sins is really happening when we find ourselves in an effective relationship with God. Even then we are not saved; we are only being saved, because we go on sinning. What Christ *did* on the Cross was not to secure a final forgiveness of our sins but to reveal the sort of God we were subject to —'a God determined not by rules of equity but by a pardon and succour that never wearies and never withholds and never spares itself'.

XIV

DEATH AND ETERNITY

Death cannot kill what never dies,
Nor can spirits ever be divided
that love and live in the same Divine Principle,
the Root and Record of their Friendship.
If Absence be not Death, neither is theirs.
WILLIAM PENN

In the belief in immortality the rationality
of the universe is at stake.
B. H. STREETER

MOST OF US live most of our lives without confronting the fact of death. This is probably a merciful dispensation. But the one certainty in life is death, and we only realize its utter finality when we have seen the life-spirit pass from a beloved countenance and know that all is changed for ever. Is this body, we ask, all that there is and ever was? Can life be explained only in biological terms? Or is there part of life that escapes such definition? That loving, lively pulsating something that we once knew to animate this cold body — is all that gone too, except as we may recall it through the channels of recollection? We do not know. As with arguments seeking to prove the existence of a personal God, there is no kind of proof yet presented that enforces intellectual acceptance of a future life. All mental pictures of life beyond the grave, from the crudest to the most sublime and desirable, remain within the realm of wishful fantasy. Pursue every known way of knowing in the realms of science and philosophy and we return empty from our quest. The dead we can see; what follows no man has seen.

But to say there is no *proof* is not to say that there are no grounds for hope. We can believe where we cannot prove if there is sufficient evidence for our encouragement. For a large part of my life I have wavered between the conviction that the facts are weighted against any other assumption than that of final extinction

107

of the spirit with the body, and a more optimistic belief that this may not be true. Conceptions of heaven as a place of reward and judgment have not impressed me; non-Christian views of the eternal chain of birth and rebirth on the wheel of Karma seemed to me no more than a plausible explanation of what cannot be explained. For long I have been content to accept the minimum belief — that immortality has no connection with survival after death but consists in the total store of memorable value bequeathed to us from the lives of good men. Briefly, that individual immortality is the continuation in us of the lives of those who have passed before us into the valley of the shadow.

There is comfort and inspiration in this belief, and some would say it is enough. I remember as an undergraduate being deeply satisfied with H. G. Wells in his 'theological' period, when his *God The Invisible King* had considerable appeal to a war-ridden generation. He thus summarized his view of immortality:

'Whether we live for ever or die tomorrow does not affect righteousness. Many people seem to find the prospect of a final personal death unendurable. This impresses me as egotism. I have no such appetite for a separate immortality; what, of me, is identified with God, is God; what is not, is of no more permanent value than the snows of yester-year.'

Many years after reading this passage, which for long appealed to my youthful idealism as a noble and generous philosophy, I read B. H. Streeter's judgment on it: 'The disinterestedness', he says, 'which is content with a Universe in which his ego will soon cease to be, is much to the credit of Mr Wells; it would not be to God's credit were He equally content.'

This brilliant comment started me thinking again. Streeter enabled me to see that it is not a question of *our* opinion concerning our individual worth, but a question of what sort of universe we are living in, and of what sort of Power rules it. Do we live in a universe ruled by an It who 'treats the individuality of heroic souls like oyster-shells at a banquet, whisked from the table to make room for the next course?' Are the heroisms, nobilities and sublime sacrifices we see expressed by the human spirit of so little value that they count for no more than the mayfly fluttering for a day over the indifferent waters of a pond? A Power who created man, we should reasonably assume, will at least accord such respect to these values as is given to them by men. And, unless Christ is a happy accident in an aimless roll of evolutionary forces, then we must assume that God is at least as good as Christ, for, as Streeter says, no creative mind can produce something higher and nobler than itself. Is it not likely, therefore, that God cares for the spirits He has made as Christ cared for them?

Although, we must confess, we have not ever found a proof of survival after death, have we not been led to believe that such a belief is not nonsensical? The point at which we have arrived is this: that it is impossible to have a belief about survival after death independently of other more general beliefs about the nature of God, the person of Christ and the nature of man. We must make our choice. If we cannot believe in a rational universe but only in a purposeless universe, if we cannot believe in a God who in ways difficult for us to grasp is a Person, if we cannot believe that the intrinsic nature of this Person is portrayed in Christ, then we cannot believe in survival after death. But if we can believe these things, then we may at least think it possible that belief in personal survival in the Beyond is not wishful thinking.

At this point we are confronted with a further challenge, thus stated by Streeter: 'In the belief in immortality the rationality of the Universe is at stake.' If there be a God who cares, and in whom reason prevails, is it conceivable that divine Reason can consent to our mortal lives being 'rounded with a sleep' after they have so often, in great men and small, borne witness to the eternal values that do not die?

But beyond all argument there is also an assurance that flows to us through the deeper channels of suffering. The Cross may teach where logic fails. Here I must return to my experience of living daily with a very dear person who I knew was going to die. I saw a lovely spirit increasingly abound in grace and power as the poor body wasted over the long months. And I gradually came to know that I was confronted with a Reality that had no place in time, but was the flowering of an eternal quality that could not die. We may live in the assurance that life will not separate us from the love of God; but can we live in an equal certainty that death may not so separate us? Through the painful revelation that comes of thus facing the close fact of death, I have come to believe it unlikely that God will destroy the souls that draw their lives from His.

And death reminds us that eternity begins now. It must be the light on life's opportunity, not death's shadow, that we choose for our guide. 'The problem for us', says John Oman, 'especially as life goes on and the horizon narrows around us, is how to live in the power of an endless life, with courage not damped and vision not darkened, interests not diminished and tasks still done as though they and we are eternal.' Whatever lies for us in the Beyond, whatever our hopes and our fears, let us face the life we know with 'eagerness for what is good to know and gratitude for what is fair to behold'.

XV

SCIENCE AND RELIGION

*'We have to build the spiritual world out of symbols taken from our
own personality, as we build the scientific world out of the symbols of
the mathematician. I think, therefore, we are not wrong in embodying
the significance of the spiritual world to ourselves in the feeling of a
personal relationship, for our whole approach to it is bound up with those
aspects of consciousness in which personality is centred.'*
ARTHUR S. EDDINGTON

'Let both grow together until the harvest.'
MATTHEW XIII, 30

'I AM ABSOLUTELY convinced', a bright sixth-former once said to
me, 'that in my life-time science will have explained away God.'
Possibly as a result of faulty divinity lessons, this devoted young
scientist had made two assumptions commonly made by many
thinking men and women. The first, that through science and the
scientific method all that there is to know can and will be made
known; the second, that inevitably science and religion must
remain in opposed and warring camps. These assumptions have
always puzzled me. When some new and revolutionary theory
of the physical universe bursts upon us I accept it as a new wonder
in the sphere to which it belongs. Similarly, the contributions
made by psychology to our knowledge of human personality
have always seemed to me to be valuable explanations of how
we 'tick', but not serious enemies to religious belief. Psychology
has explained many mysteries of human behaviour, but it has not
explained them away. It has, indeed, been the scholarly examination of the validity of the Bible, much more than the advancement
of scientific knowledge, that has led me to revise and modify my
beliefs about Christianity.

Both science and religion pursue truth; but they pursue different
categories of truth; their search is governed by different methods,
and their findings are expressed in entirely different modes. Our
sixth-form boy had gone wrong because he believed that science

could reveal all truth instead of all of a particular aspect of it; and the persecutors of Galileo and Copernicus went wrong because they assumed that religion was capable of revealing all truth including the nature of the physical universe. We get into difficulties when either scientist or priest claims a knowledge unattainable by the methods he uses in his own sphere of activity.

But it should not be assumed that because religion and science are engaged in the discovery of different kinds of truth by different methods, that the truths they reveal are entirely unrelated to each other. No truths discoverable by human genius can be thus separated into unrelated or conflicting categories. The only sensible attitude is to regard these separately discovered revelations as complementary aspects of what is to be known. This is the only way of avoiding wasteful conflict and ultimate falsity in our conclusions.

A.   CAUSES OF CONFLICT

Nevertheless, the issue is not quite so simple as this. To avoid conflict another condition has to be satisfied. The complementary nature of scientific and religious truths will not be maintained if the scientist or the 'religious' man is content with limited or spurious interpretations of the evidence available. Poor scientific thinking and poor religious thinking will not mix; neither will sound scientific conclusions consort happily with ill-considered religious conviction, or unsound scientific interpretations with 'pure religion and undefiled'.

There can be no reconciliation, for instance, between Christian fundamentalism and science. To accept the Bible as the very word of God in the sense that it is to remain untouched by scholarly criticism, that it is equally valid and inspired in all its parts, is to deny truth and to destroy the value and glory of the Bible as a religious literature. Even a milder fundamentalism that fears to relinquish traditionalist views of the Scriptures concerning the authorship of the various books, for example, and adheres to an unjustifiably simple interpretation of this vastly complex literature, does no good service to religious faith. No valid purpose is served by regarding allegory and parable as history, or the creation story as sound geology or astronomy, nor need the credibility of the Old Testament rest on the edibility of Jonah. Little but spiritual poverty comes from such literal rendering of Bible texts and no self-respecting scientist should be expected to accept so pathetic a presentation of religious belief.

But there are also similarly meagre interpretations of science. There is the view of the materialist that nothing exists except matter. The error here is that the man who makes this assertion has no right to claim more than that in the realm of knowledge in which the physicist works nothing seems to exist except matter. If then, he extends his assertion to the whole realm of existence he makes an unjustifiable assertion, and one that few physicists would now make. On the other hand, the man who declares that science deals only with matter has no necessary quarrel with religion because he is not thereby denying the existence of another realm of knowing about which science has nothing to say.

Another removable cause of conflict between science and religion arises from the view that science can give a satisfying and complete explanation of all physical and human phenomena. This 'scientific world-outlook', outside of which its upholders say there can be no other kind of 'world-outlook', leads to a deterministic view of human life. By determinism we mean that all events, whether in the physical universe or in the behaviour of human beings, are determined by causes, that is, by prior events. Opposed to this is the religious view that men have free-will, that they can sin and that they are, at least in varying degrees, responsible for their actions. Undoubtedly in the enclosed realm in which science operates it can be proved empirically, that is, by observation and experiment, that events are due to causes. Furthermore, science can predict with great accuracy what will happen in the future when the present situation is known. But in the realm of human behaviour, although we can make rough forecasts of what may happen *if* certain conditions are fulfilled, we can only make guesses as to the ultimate results, sometimes good guesses, but that is all.

In his book, *Religion and the Scientific Outlook*, a recent and most lucid contribution to this subject, T. R. Miles suggests that Shakespearean tragedy provides examples of the determinist position as it affects human affairs. Even in real life, he says, by reflecting on past events we can easily assume their inevitability: 'Things have happened, inevitably, in the one way that they did happen, and we seem powerless to alter them in much the same way as Othello is powerless to avoid murdering Desdemona.' Is this the miserable prospect for us all — that we are racing on to inevitable conclusions of success, failure or death? The crucial question that we need to ask, says T. R. Miles, is whether real life is or is not like the drama-situation (in which Othello is not told in advance how he will behave), and whether people, after being warned about their future behaviour, are or are not powerless to prevent it. This is a matter which can be settled only by an appeal to evidence; and so long as we are not ignoring important empirical discoveries we are perfectly justified in concluding that real life is sometimes *unlike* the drama-situation; that in real life people are sometimes *able* to avoid dangers about which they have been warned. It would indeed be very difficult for the determinist to prove that given a foreknowledge of what *might* happen if we do not mend our ways, we are *all* nevertheless incapable of changing the direction of our lives by an act of will.

However, we are bound to agree that the determinist can present some factors in 'real life' that seem to support his view with some degree of plausibility. We have only to look around us in our homes, schools, hospitals and prisons to see many adults and children suffering from physical and social disabilities that undoubtedly reduce or destroy their capacity to choose and act freely. Among these are abnormal glandular secretions and brain lesions that affect personality; on the environmental side are grossly defective social conditions, children deprived of maternal care, for instance, whose love-deprivation in infancy leads to the affectionless child and the young delinquent, incapable, or only partially capable, of living anything but anti-social lives. And beyond these empirically ascertainable factors that inhibit the full exercise of free-will we must take into consideration the massive impact of social conditioning that operates on all our lives, rendering us all rather less free to act with reason and responsibility.

We agree, then, that we are not always the free agents we sometimes think ourselves to be. But all that we need concede to the determinist view is that our behaviour is *sometimes* determined to a greater or less degree. We have no reason to accept the major contention that our actions are *always* determined to a complete degree. The religious man, then, whether he be scientist, layman or priest, has nothing to fear from the determinist argument. But he has something to learn. The facts of our human condition revealed by the scientist demand from us the exercise of a more enlightened moral responsibility towards sinners, a responsibility better manifested in humility and charity than in judgment and condemnation.

B. COMPLEMENTARY TRUTHS

So far I have attempted to explain in a layman's way why the cruder religious and scientific attitudes may easily come into conflict. We now have to ask in what ways the truths revealed by science and religion respectively are complementary to each other, each partial revelations of the whole truth. This is what Einstein says about the relationship of science and religion:

'Science is the century-old endeavour to bring together by means of systematic thought the perceptible phenomena of this world into as thoroughgoing an association as possible . . . religion is the age-old endeavour of mankind to become clearly and completely conscious of . . . values and goals, and constantly to strengthen and extend their effects. . . . If one conceives of religion and science according to these definitions, then a conflict between them appears impossible. For science can only ascertain what is, but not what should be, and outside its domain value judgments of all kinds remain necessary. Religion on the other hand, deals only with evaluation of human thought and action; it cannot justifiably speak of facts and relationship between facts.'

Here, then, out of the mind of the greatest scientist and mathematician of this age comes the firm declaration of the complementarity of science and religion. Science deals with facts; religion is concerned with values; and both are essential to a fuller knowledge of what there is to know. This seems to me a far more acceptable view of the relative functions of science and religion than that held by some scientists that science cannot exist without the element of value creeping into scientific judgments. Here, surely, science is being confused with the scientist, who is free, as a man, to apply value-judgments to the results of any of his activities. But this should not mean that the science in which he is engaged, or the methods of science he uses to discover new facts, are intrinsically involved with values. The scientist, it is true, may engage upon a piece of research with what can well be called religious fervour, but he would be a poor scientist who allowed enthusiasm to obscure his final allegiance to facts. The value-judgments enter in when the facts are known, at which point the scientist ceases to think as a scientist and begins to think as a layman. The fact that as a scientist he can explain the colours of the spectrum in scientific terms does not prevent his entry into another dimension which enables him to appreciate the beauty of a rainbow. Of beauty and charity science has nothing to say. But the scientist may have views about beauty and he may be searching for ways by which his knowledge may benefit mankind. It is worth noting, for instance, that the most impressive opposition to the use of the hydrogen bomb has come from nuclear physicists. At this point the scientist enters the realm of values, and when he does so he becomes involved in purposes that extend beyond his professional rôle.

C. TWO WAYS OF KNOWING

So far we have suggested that science and religion are two complementary activities that reveal complementary aspects of knowledge; the former being concerned with ascertainable facts, the latter with values. We now have to inquire into the ways these facts and values are made known, and also into the means and terminology used by scientists on the one hand and prophets, saints and theologians on the other, to communicate the truths they believe they have discovered.

It is not quite true to say that science is empirical and inductive, that scientific knowledge develops out of a continuing process of observation and rigidly controlled experiment. For science

also proceeds deductively, the scientist framing workable hypo-
theses and testing them by experiment. But whichever way he
proceeds the results are expressed in terms of quantity; his
findings are usually measurable, and, if not strictly measurable,
then at least describable in meticulous terminology, understandable
at least to the initiated. If the physicist, for instance, cannot see
his atoms pounding about according to the laws atoms obey, he
can nevertheless accurately describe what atoms do, how they
react in given circumstances, by his observations of the results of
these reactions. To communicate and explain what happens he
uses symbols that describe these physical relationships in terms of
quantity and activity. And he can do this with such precision that
by obeying the laws he has discovered he can produce atom
bombs, sputniks or fertilisers by reproducing the respective
relationships required. This means of communication, of explanation, is diagrammatic rather than pictorial. If he allowed values to
enter into his calculations he would fail.

Lest, in my ignorance of science, I should be over-simplifying
the true nature of science and the means of scientific communication, I thought it best to discuss these problems with a scientist
friend, who is particularly concerned with the philosophy of
science. I found that I had in fact over-simplified the issue,
particularly in my reference to 'facts' and 'measurement'. But
on the whole his view agreed with mine. He explained the
situation something like this:

'By suggesting that science is the observation of sense-
perceived phenomena, we say at once too much and too little.
Too much, because science is not concerned with the sense-
perception of great pictorial art or great music; too little,
because beyond its sense-perceptions, which can roughly be
regarded as the elements of its experiments and experiences,
science has its wonderful conceptual systems, e.g. the molecular
theory in chemistry, the quantum theory in physics. The great
controversies of science are usually concerned not with facts
but with theories.

Again, if mathematics is the language of science, as some
say it is, then this suggests that science is essentially metrical
and confined to that which can be measured. To say that

science is measurement is nonsense as it stands; it is like saying "I see" but declining to answer the question "What do I see?" But if we ask "What kind of a thing does science study?" the question can at least partially be answered in Martin Buber's language: the scientist's chief interest is the

It — It world

not the I — It

nor the I — Thou world

And the "Its" in which the scientist is interested have no moral or artistic value. His concepts are constructions of his own mind, and sometimes they are fully mathematical. Yet they are not utterly independent of his experience; but are — quite mysteriously — suggested by it. Some concepts of science are not mathematical at all, for example, the concept of the chemical element. Pasteur's wonderful asymmetric objects were more like conceptual diagrams.'

And then my friend adds a significant footnote:

'When we come to a great conceptual system, such as that of Newton's dynamics of masses moving in absolute space and time, we have come to something very like the fruitful myths of religion. These myths may be so true, that any attempt to make them less mythical makes them less true. When Einstein builds again on Newton's ground, he creates a new myth. The absolute truth seems as unattainable in science as in any other field of knowledge.'

With the possible exception of the use of myth to express concepts that defy more precise definition, we come upon a quite different situation when we turn to the 'findings' of religion. It is not quantity but quality that is involved, not mathematical or diagrammatic definition but the blurred though suggestive strokes of the artist that convey meaning, not measurements but values that are up for assessment. The nearest approach to scientific method that we find in the pursuit of moral values is the testing of a moral hypothesis by attempting to live in accordance with it. (See page 50). Thus the methods of discovery and the means of communication used in the pursuit of moral and religious truths are more akin to art than to science. The artist is not concerned to convey knowledge; his is an activity which engages his inner life in an attempt to portray life as it appears to him. And he expresses himself in terms of picture, poem, story, parable and even myth, as he becomes conscious of the inner meaning of all Life. That is what Eddington means when he says that 'we have to build the spiritual world out of symbols taken from our own personality'. 'Art', says Streeter 'is *par excellence* the method by which we are made to feel quality beyond the limits of our own experience, by entering into an experience finer, deeper or wider than our own.'

It is not an accident, then, that so much of what the religious man holds to be truth he has expressed in poetry and parable whose object is to arouse in us inner experiences which no cold statement of fact could ever evoke. A catalogue of the attributes of God will leave us unmoved or unconvinced; the parable of the prodigal son stirs a response in us which becomes an *experience* of the quality of love the parable is intended to convey. Thus the 'evidences' for religious truth are not part of philosophical or theological argument; they are rather the effect of the presentations of religious truth on our inward life, the quality of this life being observable only through the quality of our personality and conduct. The personality of the religious man, says Streeter, 'is the only real expression of religion'.

Let us now consider two examples of the use of myth and parable in the expression of religious truth. First, the creation myth. As a statement of historical fact it is false. But this is unimportant. As a declaration of God's unity with all physical phenomena and human life it is of supreme importance, for it makes us look at the physical creation and our neighbour in a particular way. We are turned away from fearful contemplation of uncontrollable chaos to a realization of spiritual power, order and purpose, behind the universe and in the daily round of living. This conception of God's relation to man and the physical universe affects our lives. If we accept the message we are bound to do something about it.

What we have to do is described in the language of parable, which uses the symbols of personality, the 'aspects of consciousness in which personality is centred', to convey meaning. The parable of the prodigal son, for example, is a moving revelation of divine and human relationships — of the loving Father to his children, of brethren to one another, of the means to reconciliation in repentance and forgiveness. There is not a word in the parable that fails to touch an intimate chord in human experience. If we accept the parable we commit ourselves to a way of life in which the Father's love is expressed through our attitudes and activities. We become *engaged* in the expression of love in all its manifestations of neighbourliness, reconciliation, restraint of judgment — the world over. And Christianity is just that — the establishment of right human relationships.

But the atheist may say that he cannot accept the validity of the parable because we can present no proof that God exists or that He is loving. The atheist cannot prove that we are wrong, neither can we prove that we are right. T. R. Miles, in the work already referred to, thus helps us out of the dilemma:

'What is clear is that it is foolish to condemn a self-professed atheist or regard him as missing something important in life until we know what his attitude to life really is. We can discover this attitude if we know what parables he tells. If it is said that an atheist is one who does not accept any parable at all, my comment would be this: all of us alike are confronted with the question how we ought to live; and, whatever way of life we choose, we can be said to be implicitly accepting one set of parables or another. If the parable we accept is not that of a loving father, it is likely to be that of a purposeless world, indifferent or actively hostile to man's highest endeavours. Such a parable cannot be shown to be wrong. But to live in accordance with it involves a commitment no less than does living in accordance with the theistic parable. The self-professed atheist or agnostic may not explicitly have made such a commitment; but all living involves acceptance of one parable or another.'

The choice of our parable, then, is a matter of personal and moral conviction. We choose and take the consequences. And our choice will not be founded on what we 'know' in the scientist's sense of knowing; it is based rather on a way of 'knowing' that is more akin to belief than knowledge. It is the sense in which Job used the phrase 'Now I know', which was the conviction that he had at last found a way of living, firmly founded on his personal experience but quite unprovable in the way the mathematician proves things.

D. PSYCHOLOGY

The definitions we have applied to the pure sciences are less applicable to the life-sciences, biology, physiology and psychology. This is most evident in psychology which in some of its branches is strictly metrical in method, in others, in psychotherapy, for example, the approach is intuitive and sympathetic, more a matter of imaginative insight than of scientific precision. The psychiatrist's method of communication is more akin to the language of parable, and he works very close to the border-line that divides facts from values, easily moving from the one to the other in the course of his diagnosis and cure of mental illness. We owe an immense debt to the psychologist and neurologist who, by enlarging our knowledge of the mechanisms of the human mind, have released men from many ills and terrors. But it is difficult to see how knowledge of the way our minds work replaces our need for moral and religious guidance. Psychology has served religion well in exploring the hidden motive and destroying harmful superstition; but it has yet to be proved that it has explained away the need for moral choice.

The eminent neurologist and psychologist, Sir Russell Brain, thus sums up the matter:

'The main function which psychology can perform for the individual is to enable him to know himself better, and to see more clearly the way in which his thinking and feeling are influenced by unconscious motives, and, so far as he sees this, to make allowance for it and correct it, and to recognize the limitation and partiality of his point of view even when thus corrected. The man who has applied this discipline to himself will thereby understand others better, for he will recognize in them the mental processes he has discovered to exist in himself. But in all this the function of psychology is a negative one, to use a surgical term it is orthopaedic, corrective of deformity. It will enable a man to walk better, but it will not tell him where to walk. He must look elsewhere for a dynamic.'

E. LET BOTH GROW TOGETHER

I may have simplified the issues, but I have attempted to define them as they appear to me. There are no doubt subtleties of judgment and definition I may have missed; contradictions still unresolved. Yet, as A. N. Whitehead says in *Science and the Modern World*, 'In formal logic a contradiction is the sign of defeat; but in the evolution of real knowledge it marks the first step in progress towards a victory.' It is not the contradictions that matter so much as the integrity and open-mindedness with which we pursue truth, at no point turning away in pride or cocksureness that our way of knowledge is the only way. The point at issue between the scientist and the 'religious man' is whether there is only one way of knowing. The need is that each should recognize both the validity and the necessity of the two ways of knowing. For the rest —'let both grow together until the harvest', and it is likely, when the sickle comes, that neither the tares nor the wheat will be found exclusively in the fields of science or the fields of religion.

As far as my personal belief is concerned I have found it easier to come to the conclusions here outlined because I approached the problem not from the background of an authoritarian belief but from a religion of experience. Arthur S. Eddington's comment that 'Quakerism with its absence of creeds holds out a hand to the scientist', is valid also for the layman. Credal formulation of belief, valuable in its conserving influence as it is, nevertheless presents obstacles to the free acceptance of new evidence that may seem at first glance to shake the Church's foundation. That is at least one reason why Friends have effortlessly accepted new advances in scientific knowledge, regarding them as further manifestations of God's glory rather than as hindrances to belief. Arthur S. Eddington's regular attendance at the Friends' Meeting at Cambridge, of which he was a member, has often appealed to me as a happy symbol of the ease with which a great scientist may sit among ordinary folk 'waiting for God to break through'.

PART III

Applications

XVI

ORGANIZING INDIVIDUALS

'Dearly beloved Friends, these things we do not lay upon you as a rule or form to walk by; but that all, with the measure of light which is pure and holy, may be guided: and so in the light walking and abiding, these things may be fulfilled in the Spirit, not from the letter, for the letter killeth, but the Spirit giveth life.'

MEETING OF ELDERS AT BALBY
YORKSHIRE, 1656

IT HAS BEEN my lot over many years to attend innumerable committees and to have taken part in voting on many hundreds of issues. To look back on this experience, to occasions when a single vote has decided the matter, yields me little satisfaction. So often the minority remained frustrated; and how often the minority might have been right! To have discovered in Friends' conduct of their business affairs a quite different procedure has been a pleasant experience. I want, therefore, to say something about organization and Friends' ways of conducting secular affairs, for they seem to offer possibilities of usefulness beyond the confines of the Society.

No other single experience of Quaker ways has more attracted me than their manner of conducting the business of the Society in their committees and meetings. Here I found groups of ordinary people, in varying walks of life and of greatly differing capacities, who were actually practising in the act of discussion the very heart of the belief that informed their religious convictions. This struck me as at least unusual. It seemed to be the more remarkable because Quakerism places so much emphasis on the right of individuals to have and to express their own opinions. One might have thought this would be a formidable obstacle to the harmony of many wills. But, on the contrary, I discovered a most seemly balance between individual freedom and corporate unity, secured without any suppression of minority opinion and in a strikingly self-disciplined way, in which a

125

willingness to be influenced by the views of others was most evident. Whether it were a question of finance, planning study groups, decorating the meeting house or a deeper matter of faith and discipline, the same spirit prevailed. There was no coercion of any kind, no voting, no raised voices, no heat, although there might have been a deep vocal appeal, and as far as I have been able to judge seldom a decision made that did not secure general approval. Quite early on in my experiences of business meetings I began to realize that there was an Influence greater than the will of any person present that exerted its discipline over all. How did this come about? How have Friends managed to organize people in this seemly and satisfactory way? The answer is to be found in the slow growth of traditions solidly founded on the conviction that human institutions as well as persons must be governed by 'that of God which joins us together'.

Quakerism began as a movement; the object of Fox and his fellow workers was to purify and simplify Christian practice, not to form a separate and protesting branch of the church. But it becomes the fate of most religious movements, in their effort to preserve precious gains, to establish a visible organization which results in the emergence of a new sect. This happened to the Quaker movement; which became the Society of Friends. It was inevitable that this should have happened. Increasing numbers, the isolation of widely scattered groups, the claims of the persecuted and their dependants on the care of Friends, but above all the sense of sharing a common experience, all pointed towards the need for closer cohesion. As early as 1654 we find Fox's practical mind facing this problem by forming regular local meetings of Friends; in 1658 we hear of a Yearly General Meeting. In 1675 appeared the Meeting for Sufferings, which met regularly to succour Friends in gaol. Our central executive monthly committee still meets in London and bears that name. Gradually there emerged the structure of 'Meetings' with which we are familiar today — Preparative, Monthly, Quarterly and Yearly Meetings — through which the Society expresses its corporate witness as a religious community. It is through this simple organization, little changed for three hundred years, that the Society conducts its business.

The Monthly Meeting, grouping several local Preparative

Meetings for worship, is the central administrative and delibera-
tive body, for Friends have been chary of relying too much on
congregational autonomy. The larger meetings, Quarterly and
Yearly, exist to bring the affairs of the Society into a wider
national and international range, and to deal with matters beyond
the capacity of the smaller groups. Individual Friends bear the
burden of responsibility for the decisions of any meeting they
attend; the least member in the Church, says Fox, 'hath an office
and is serviceable and every member hath need one of another'.
In this nice balance between the freedom of individuals and the
orderly conduct of the Society's affairs, Friends have been able
to achieve throughout their community a unity of mind free
from inhibiting uniformity, and scope for individual initiative
free from the danger of anarchy.

This unity and freedom, nevertheless, owe more to the spirit
informing Friends' use of their simple organization than to its
actual structure. The Quaker approach to secular affairs is directly
derived from their religious convictions. It is not so much a
method that is used as an attitude of mind that governs method.
Belief in the Inward Light inevitably leads to firm belief in the
importance of persons; the conviction that worship begins in
communication with the Holy Spirit but extends into fellowship
with our neighbour, makes of all secular affairs an extension of the
religious life into the worldly life. Hence, every meeting for the
conduct of business affairs is a meeting for worship and is held
in that spirit, whether it be a gathering of a thousand people at
Yearly Meeting or a small group of five or six Friends. Success
is achieved only when their deliberations are governed by a tender
regard for the leadings of all Friends present.

In practice the Clerk of the Meeting presides; but his function
is to listen and to guide rather than to lead or dominate. Final
decisions rest with the meeting. Every member present is equally
free to speak and to suggest, for it is not assumed that wisdom is
the monopoly of a few. Where the right spirit prevails each
contribution is received with respect and successive speakers will
build on what has gone before, striving to remember that they
are not there to enforce their own opinions but to seek true
solutions. There is no room for debate, nor even for argument.
It is rather a matter of pooling resources. There is no voting, for

the counting of heads involves the suppression of the minority, and in any case, it is assumed that there is neither majority nor minority, but only a united group of people desiring a right decision.

How then are decisions made? It is here that the Clerk performs a difficult but important function. It is his task to assess the 'sense of the meeting', that is, to form a judgment on the total trend of opinion, and ultimately to frame a minute which satisfies the whole gathering. Sometimes his task is easy; sometimes it is baffling; in which case he may ask Friends to pause for a brief period of worship so that unity may emerge from silent prayer. If honest views remain unreconciled the matter may have to be adjourned to a later occasion.

This method of doing business may seem to be cumbersome; it can certainly be time-consuming. But it has many advantages which Friends believe outweigh its shortcomings. In the first place, the outcome is seldom a mere compromise, the least common denominator of conflicting opinions. Most often the decision arrived at is more comprehensive and satisfying than any single proposal put forward by an individual. This is because the meeting has pooled its resources and because minds have remained open to convincement. How often have I attended business meetings with what I thought were the right answers, only to find that the corporate sense of the meeting had a far better and richer answer than I had. Again, no one is hurt. The decision is unanimous. There is no remaining soreness from the oppressive weight of the majority. Hence every person is willing to implement the corporate will because it is also his. The discussion has been educative when we have been willing to see the value of opinions different from our own, and when we have been glad to see our limited ideas developed by those of others. The method is indeed slow, but it usually yields lasting results.

Thus while individuals have complete freedom to bring their ideas and concerns to the group, they do so in the knowledge that there is a wider group-wisdom which will not be repressive but which is just as likely to enrich and extend the original concern as to modify or reject it. The group is chiefly concerned to ensure that all are guided by what is consistent with Quaker testimony to Christian truth, and that individual and group activity, both in purpose and performance, have their roots in neighbourly love and reconciliation.

In the wider life of the meeting the preservation of this spirit is a general responsibility of the membership, but in the absence of an ordained minister, certain persons are given particular pastoral duties. Among these are the Elders, chosen for their experience and personal capacity, who are concerned for the spiritual vitality of the meeting, for the right holding of the meeting for worship, for the quality of the vocal ministry, for the encouragement of the timid and the young to join in the spoken ministry, and even for the gentle restraint of those who, on rare occasions, may abuse or disturb the freedom and purpose of the meeting for worship. But, fully interpreted, the responsibilities of Elders extend beyond the oversight of ministry. Far more important is the nurturing of the spiritual resources of the whole membership, so that through their own awakened minds and prayerfulness, they encourage study and stimulate the spiritual life of the meeting into greater depth and power. No meeting need worry about its quality if Friends are alive and on their spiritual feet. Today Elders have a special responsibility for the young whose idealism is confronted with bewildering assaults, not only from the electronic world but from many most persuasive agnostic moralities.

To Overseers is given the 'oversight' of the flock. It is their duty to exercise pastoral care over the whole membership, to visit the sick, to assist those distressed with personal problems and to ensure that the educational needs of the children are satisfied. They will also keep in touch with members whose continued absence from meeting for worship may be due to indifference or to dissatisfaction with their meeting.

Thus the institutions of Eldership and Oversight illustrate once again the balance existing between individual freedom and the preservation of corporate unity. There is no question here of leaders and led. Through the unobtrusive performance of their duties Elders may exercise an imperceptible discipline, which leaves individuals free to think and speak as they will while tending to encourage what all desire, namely, an active harmony of attitude in which all have a part. This gentle discipline of the group over the individual, and the sense of complete freedom from group pressure which each individual feels, I have found to be a most refreshing experience. One should be able to enter any Quaker gathering, large or small, with the confidence that every man and woman present is under a responsibility to respect persons, and that this obligation will be honoured within the limits of human frailty. A touching example of the relationship between the 'weighty' Friend and the untried beginner is seen in the following incident far back in Quaker annals. At a large gathering attended by William Penn and several leading Friends, it was expected that these elders would carry the main burden of the meeting, but it was a young unknown Friend who was its inspiration. Penn said to him afterwards 'the main part of the service of this day's work went on thy side and we saw it and were willing and easy to give way to the truth, though it was through thee, who appears but like a shrub, and it is but reasonable the Lord should make use of whom he pleases'.

Another instance of the gentle disciplinary pressures of Quakerism is the use of the Advices and Queries to remind us of the obligations involved in membership of a religious society. Knowing, in their common-sensical way, how easy it is to be cumbered about with the petty affairs of daily routine to the neglect of the deep roots from which the good life springs, Friends have from early days taken steps to remind themselves of their shortcomings. The means they have adopted have varied throughout the centuries to meet changing circumstances. Today the Advices take the form of general reminders of the nature of Christian living and its implications for the daily conduct of life in society. The Queries cover similar ground but are framed in the form of questions containing a direct and personal challenge — are you actually doing this or doing that? These questions are practical and pointed and cover a wide range of Christian obligation, extending from the need for love and forgiveness to the keeping of accounts and defrauding the public revenue. Parts of the Advices and Queries are read regularly in Meeting throughout the year. In this way, Friends are challenged to examine the faithfulness of their lives in the silence, with the challenge of their accepted obligations sounding quietly in their ears.

It is often a chastening experience to measure humbly the extent of your sins of omission before queries such as these for example:

Do you cherish that of God within you, that His Power growing in you may rule your life?

Is your religion rooted in spiritual experience and does it find expression in your life?

Do you cherish a forgiving spirit? Are you careful of the reputation of others; and do you avoid and discourage tale-bearing and detraction?

Are you on your guard against the love of ease and self-indulgence?

Do you come faithfully to our meetings for worship with heart and mind prepared?

Do you, as a Church, exercise a loving care for the children and young people of your meeting?

Are you striving to develop your mental powers and to use them to the glory of God . . . do you keep your mind open to new light, from whatever quarter it may arise?

Are you honest and truthful in word and deed? Do you maintain strict integrity in your business transactions? Are you careful not to defraud the public revenue?

Do you as disciples of the Lord Jesus take a living interest in the social conditions of those around you?

Are you faithful in maintaining our testimony against all war. . . . Do you live in the life and power that takes away the occasion of all wars?

These are samples of the simple but penetrating questions touching many of those aspects of life about which ordinary men need to ask questions. The listening Friends are free to ponder or neglect them. Each Friend is his own confessor and only God can give absolution. But I believe that through these Advices and Queries there is exerted a kind of discipline that is self-imposed, free from coercion and yet effective in preserving a sense of common purpose among individuals.

Thus in their efforts to organize individuals Friends use a structure three hundred years old, which has been tried, and when imaginatively used, has not been found wanting. In practice the

Society is a pure democracy in which any member is free to take direct part without the devices of delegation or representation. No individual is relieved of responsibility; no Quaker group will coerce the individual, either by force of personality or the power of the vote. But apart from these attitudes towards persons throughout the Society there is a respect for traditional methods that exerts its own restraining influence and preserves a general harmony which never obscures a wide variety of opinion. There is a proliferation of committees, not mentioned here, each with an objective consistent with some expression of Quakerism. And throughout these various parts of Quaker organization there flows, I believe, a truly educative influence, because responsibility is widely spread and because Friends strive to accept the implications of their conviction that the Light 'shines through all'.

XVII

MARRIAGE AND THE FAMILY

'Mind that which is pure in you to join you together.'

GEORGE FOX

MY WIFE and I were married a few years before we joined the Society of Friends. During these years we were striving to find some resting place in the Christian communion, for we had fallen away from the churches of our parents and were somewhat adrift. Our entry into membership brought about a great clarification and a deepening realization of the nature of the venture to which we were committed. Married life gained in quality, we found, as Quaker teaching became excitingly relevant to all we wanted to be and to do as married persons and parents. Our intimate lives both in their physical and their spiritual expression gained in significance. We became more aware of what marriage was, of what it yielded in joy and pain, of the meaning of giving and getting, of what parenthood implied. I am not aware that we on any occasion overtly declared our knowledge of what was happening to us; the experience was too slow and the changes in our lives at any one moment were imperceptible, but this good thing happened. Only now, as I am writing, do I pause to ask why. And so what follows is the product of a long glance over my shoulder, now it is all over. On the whole I think my views are Quakerly; in any case they are views acquired in Quaker experience.

A. MARRIAGE

Of all mankind's attempts to organize social life only the family seems to have survived the test of time, maintaining a high survival value amidst influences that have destroyed empires. This is no doubt because the family is the only unit in society in which personal relationships are primarily biological. Blood binds the family unit in a unique association which no act of will can deny. That, I suppose, is why the family becomes the growing point of community and also why its preservation is of the utmost importance for the maintenance of healthy communities. In the Christian era in the West the family has been gradually elevated from an institution that reasonably fulfils various demands of ordered civil life to a divinely ordained group of relationships essential to the spiritual growth of men and women. Thus, biological in its beginnings, deeply based in the natural order of creation, the family becomes part of the divine order of creation, a means of preparing men for the disciplines and charities of life and for sonship with God.

The Christian family is firmly based on the conviction that the only true marriage is monogamous. Why is this? Such a conviction is not derived from the religious requirement that we should love our neighbour; if it were it would not be too difficult to build up a case for polygamy. Nor can it be argued that men are by nature monogamous; the facts of life do not suggest that they are. If we say that marriage is a lawful state for the procreation of children we do not thereby preclude legally established polygamous marriage. Even the argument of the manifest moral advantages for children of monogamous parents leaves unanswered the question of the involuntary childless marriage. Is the happy and otherwise fruitful union of a childless marriage without meaning and value? We shall get into endless difficulties if we try to argue that it is. We have, indeed, to discover a reason for monogamy, and also for faithfulness in marriage, that is as valid for an involuntary childless union as it is for a marriage followed by the blessing of children.

The Christian case for marriage as a life-long bond, 'for better, for worse . . . till death us do part', rests not merely on the need for order in the community but on the Christian view of the nature of man. The biological and the spiritual nature of men are each to be reckoned with in the relationships involved in marriage. Emil Brunner in *The Divine Imperative* beautifully described these relationships as a unique relationship of the trinity — father, mother, child:

'The unique element in this human existence . . . is thus bound up with two other existences. I, as a child, owe my life to these two persons. And I, as a father or a mother, with this woman or with this man, have given to this person his — human — existence. I, with this woman or with this man, have taken part in the divine miracle of creation. Not a body but a real corporeal person, a human being now stands there alongside of me as that which has come into being as the result of being united with this woman . . . since I, the father as well as the mother and the child know irrevocably that this fact is irrevocable, then we three persons have ever been bound together, in an unparalleled and indissoluble relation. The seeing eyes of all three, our mutual knowledge of one another and of this relation, hold us firmly one to another. . . . This trinity of being we call the human structure of existence.'

This is not merely a description of the physiological facts that account for the birth of a child. It belongs to the world of values, not to genetics. It is a declaration that the essence of a true marriage is the union of two personalities, not of two bodies, each of whom finds completion in the person of the other. Christian marriage, then, is not a facile means of avoiding fornication, it is not merely a state for the lawful begetting of children, it is not merely the most desirable means for rearing a family; it is rather the recognition of a divine purpose which takes us beyond physical satisfactions to a realization of the spiritual capacities of human personality.

The truly creative love between a man and a woman grows out of deep physical and spiritual affinities. Where either is lacking love is weakened. The completion of the man as a man and the woman as a woman depends on the merging of each personality in a union where body and spirit join in continuous surrender. Each gives; each partakes; personality is completed in the mergence of two bodies and two souls each the complement and fulfilment of the other, not only in the intimate and intermittent moments of physical union, but in the continuing companionship of two utterly different people, whose lives are yet bound in irrevocable identity. Such identity does not obliterate personality; it differentiates and strengthens it. The man becomes more a man; the woman more a woman.

Thus Christian marriage provides for all expressions of love. It recognizes the dual nature of sexual love; its physical beginning and spiritual completion; it insists that faithfulness and permanence are essential to its success; and by regarding marriage as a means to the spiritual growth of two persons the Christian view, I believe, places high value on the childless union. Although such a union is bound to lack the completeness of one blessed with children, it can nevertheless be a blessing to the two persons involved, and a double benediction on their friends. How often has the agony of unfulfilment in this one part of life been wonderfully transmitted into service far beyond the childless home!

One of the causes of failure in marriage is the separation of the sex life from loving responsibility for the welfare of the partner. The sex act is not love itself but one of the ways of expressing love, biologically and spiritually essential to the full love-life of a man and a woman. In the long experience of mankind, purely physical love has been proved to have within it the seeds of its own decay. This is undoubtedly because its object is too often to satisfy the 'I', not to give satisfaction to the 'Thou' of the partnership. Men and women deny the nature of their very being when they attempt to build relationships on this purely physical basis. For in the procession of continual 'takings' the well of pleasure will one day run dry, for the one or the other, and only the arid dust of memory and regret will remain. But where the *motif* of married life is 'What can I give to my loved one?' new spiritual resources are continuously released in the giving; a life of intimate communion slowly emerges where the ecstasy of physical union becomes an incident, even if a necessary incident, in the enriched life that is the service of love. It is so important to realize that the mating of two persons in sexual union is not complete if the act of surrender has no continued counterpart in the tenderness of sharing along the calmer channels of daily living — at the sink and at the breakfast table. In such a situation the tensions, the quarrels, inseparable from such an intimate association of two persons, are transformed into understanding, and make of the breaking point a stronger bond. The way to such a desirable condition may be long; but it is seldom tedious. After twenty years of married life husband and wife should find each other far more interesting people than they were in the youthful age of passion.

Clearly marriage is not a venture to be undertaken lightly. Under the violent tensions of sexual love it is easy for two young people to assume that the vital physical attraction and satisfaction is the dominant issue. On the other hand, perhaps more rarely, it may happen that two young people assume that common intellectual or aesthetic interests are sufficient foundation for marriage. In each case they are mistaken; unless both of these conditions are fulfilled marriage remains a gamble. Before marriage young people must desire each other's bodies; but they must also respect each other's minds and seek to know each other in ways distinct from bodily satisfactions. Unless they can be good companions. forgetting at times the soft pressures of the embrace in the pursuit of interests outside themselves, the future does not beckon them on. They may quarrel, but they must never be bored. In courtship boredom should be regarded as the reddest of red lights.

These views about courtship and marriage are my own, but I think they would be generally acceptable to Friends. I believe, also, but with less assurance, that my views on divorce would be shared by most members of the Society in England. There was a time early in this century when it was possible for a leading Friend to say that the Society had had no experience of divorce. That, unfortunately, could not be said today, but it is nevertheless true that divorce is rare where each partner is a Friend. This is probably due to the very real and traditional concern that Friends should contemplate marriage with a deep seriousness, and to their conviction that it is an act devoutly performed in the presence of God: 'Marriage has always been regarded by Friends as a religious, not a mere civil compact' says our *Christian Faith and Practice*. Consequently appropriate members of a Meeting, by guidance and counsel, would make devoted efforts to repair a marriage that seemed to be in danger of failing. For it is a very solemn promise that has been made, as the simple and beautiful words for the solemnization of marriage testify. In a Meeting for Worship the man and the woman say: *Friends, I take this my Friend A. B. to be my wife/husband, promising through Divine assistance, to be unto her/him a loving and faithful husband/wife, until it shall please the Lord by death to separate us.*

To make such a promise is to partake in a sacrament, and such promises should not be broken. By its nature Christian marriage is indissoluble. And by Christian marriage I mean a union in which the Christian virtues of charity and understanding are in constant exercise. Here truly 'God has joined together.' But suppose there is every evidence that these conditions do not exist; that in a devastating way what was thought to be love has turned to hate; that two persons are slowly destroying each other. Can we then say that this is a true marriage of which God is the begetter? Are there not some unions of which God did not approve no matter what holy words were pronounced at the ceremony? Are there not some marriages which are, indeed, mere ceremonies rather than solemnizations of a holy thing; wrong in the beginning rather than failing in the practice? For tortured souls there must surely be some way of release rather than condemnation to continual unhappiness. And more than that; a way of release that gives freedom to form another union likely to fructify in blessing.

I make no concession here to the light-hearted affairs of Reno, or to the sordid adulteries of sensual men and women. But I am quite sure that there are instances where divorce opens a way to repair grievous error, and to rebuild shattered lives. Nevertheless, I am aware of many difficulties. The chief of these is the problem of children. Where children are involved their happiness and interests appear to me paramount and demand the utmost sacrifices from the divided parents. To beget children is to enter upon a binding responsibility that supersedes all considerations of personal desire. The issue here involves far more than the happiness of the two parents, for the welfare of the family is at stake; a delicately articulated complex of loyalties, affections, emotional security and trust and the future stability of the children are faced with disintegration. Such a situation demands that parents should raise duty above all considerations of personal antipathy or personal desire, and strive to the uttermost for a reconciliation sufficient to preserve their children from harm. The saddest, most tragic and least excusable action is that of a parent who deserts growing children either to satisfy unworthy desire or to escape the trials of incompatibility. Nevertheless, it may be, so far as human judgment can see, that even the desertion of children may be better than the devastating influence of two warring adults in what is irrevocably a broken family circle. There comes a point where only God can know the fully wise thing to do.

B. THE FAMILY

When I was appointed to the headship of a Quaker boarding school, where it had been the tradition for the headmaster's wife to play a definite rôle, my wife firmly declared before our arrival, 'Now get this quite clear; *I'm* going to bring up my children. You can look after your boys; but I'm having no nursemaids to look after mine.' She was right, of course. Bringing up a family is a full-time job. Little children need a large part of a mother's attention.

But rearing a family is not primarily a process of constantly doing things to children; it is first and foremost *being* something to children. Parents cannot choose the children they have, but to a high degree they can decide the sort of people they themselves will be; and what they are and the quality of the bond that unites them, will largely determine the quality of their family life. I mean something quite specific in saying this, namely, that the physical and spiritual intimacies of their own private lives, the lives they live separately from their children's lives, must be emotionally satisfying. Thus they appear to be a mother-father person to their children, an identity that presents stability, peace and harmony even amidst superficial disagreement. The love that binds them thus becomes the love that binds the family. The rearing of children, then, begins not with parent-child relationships but with mother-father relationships. Hence the begetting of children should not create a shift of affection from one of the partners to the children, but a deepening of husband-wife love just because it is now extended beyond themselves to the wider circle.

It has been my experience that this strengthening of the bond, the increasing and mutual respect that emerges from troubles faced in common, is immensely helped when the partners in parenthood have what I had best call a religious attitude to life;

that is to say a quiet unspoken conviction that our lives must be guided by standards and values that have permanent and pressing significance for us. I define a religious attitude to life in this broad way because I wish to include in it as wide a range of people as possible, not merely those who make some particular religious profession of faith. Nevertheless, in our own case, we found membership of the Society of Friends a reminder that our lives were not entirely ours. In times of stress we always found in the rich quarry of Christian Quaker wisdom an answer to our bewilderments bringing with it a renewed sense of purpose, a clearer view of the distant point towards which we were hesitantly striving. And what was this distant point? It was the view we had of ourselves as parents who had to become worthy of our children's love. And looking back upon so many dismal failures I am consoled by the hope that it was, perhaps, more important for our children to see us trying than that we should succeed. Part of this discipline is well described by Harold Loukes in *Friends and Their Children*, the best book I know about the rearing of a family:

'We have to forgive each other, not for what we have done, but for what we are, for being so infinitely less than we ought to be. We have to learn to give where we had hoped to get, and to understand where we had hoped to be understood.'

Whenever a parent writes about family life it should be understood that he does not do so under the guise of a successful parent but as one who could wish to try again with his errors in mind. Alas, it is too true, that the advice we are able to give to our friends is founded largely on what we have learned from our failures. What might we have done if we knew what we know now! Nevertheless, even from the beginning, principles help, a few simple attitudes to life and to children, based on what we believe men and children to be. We shall make mistakes, and because of our imperfections we shall leave scars which may take long to heal. Fortunately for parents there is an autonomy in children that helps them to heal themselves, and a resilience that is self-protective. Our chief task is to discover as far as we may what is God's pattern for them and help them to conform to that rather than to our own.

The simple essentials of Quaker belief have helped me profoundly in forming working principles for the rearing of children. As a schoolmaster and parent I found myself turning to them for general guidance increasingly as the years went by, because I discovered them to be quite practical guides in difficult situations. This sense of direction was derived from the concept of the Seed of God in human personality, a belief that compels us first to respect persons and then to recognize the capacity of young people to assist in their own development. Attitudes to discipline are necessarily transformed by such a view. This respect for persons in its turn demands from the controlling adult a tender regard for growing personality, a recognition of a child's need to be himself, to grow according to his true pattern, assisted by our guidance but not twisted into a shape conformable to our convenience. Again, the Quaker emphasis on inner experience, on making truth and opinion our own, commits us to methods aiming at the release of innate capacities rather than at the imposition of the second-hand. Obedience is slowly allowed to emerge as the result of experimentation with growing insights and becomes a way of acquiring a self-imposed conduct of life.

There is no suggestion here that from birth children should take charge while parents trot on hopefully but fearfully one step behind. The first need of a child is to feel that he lives in a world of stable values. He needs, Susan Isaacs reminds us, to feel that the adults around him are stronger than he is, for this makes him feel safe, even in his tantrums. There are times when he *needs* to feel that he can be *made* to do things, and that his parents are controlled guides and reliable supports in his many frustrating experiences. In this way he learns to adapt his impulses to a real world. Genetic psychology supports Pestalozzi's guess that a child *needs* to learn to obey because in this way he learns 'that he is not here only for his own sake'. Neither Quakerism nor modern psychology provide evidence for the belief that little children need or can make use of complete freedom. There must be rules about bed-time and meal-times and quiet assumptions about washing up. There must be firm insistence that certain things have to be done: 'Off you go to bed, and don't argue.'

It is, indeed, in the practice of obedience that children become free, for it is from mild and tempered disciplines that they learn to govern their frustrating desires. But mere external restraint is never enough to build-up the self-disciplines that make us really free. Gradually children have to learn to appreciate the relevance to their own needs of rules proposed to them, so that they move on from obedience to commands they do not readily understand to obedience that is understood. This is really part of the process of weaning that goes on throughout life as we pass out of parental control into self-control, a process, of course, that is never completed. Our ultimate object, then, our distant point, should be to enable our children to obey themselves. Then they are free. Grow up, grow up, is the spur they need.

How easy to write is this advice; how hard to practise! Truly here is the point at which all the artist in parent or teacher is called upon. The key-word is responsibility. It is by accepting responsibility that children grow up. Slowly and with discretion we have to thrust responsibility on them. Young people are easily surfeited with advice; they usually love responsibility, and it is by accepting it, just as much as they can bear, that they grow up by standing on their own feet and liking the feel of the new ground they stand on. When responsibility is consciously felt, and the response to it is successfully accomplished, personality begins to grow. Hence whatever word, act, attitude or sign of inner prompting emerges from the core of a child's moral capacity, like a tender shoot from a dormant branch, this we are called upon to cultivate. For now the time has come when it is not *our* conscience, *our* intuition we are to impose on him; our aim is to liberate *his* will, so that feeling his own will at work he comes to know where his responsibility lies. This is real inner experience, the beginning of knowledge of ourselves. And it is the beginning also of religious experience, which as we grow older extends from the first little daily decisions in which responsibility was first exercised into wider and richer realms of choice and duty.

Hence, in our dealings with children there always comes a point where adult insistence should stop so that a child's will may work. Teachers and parents should always be watching for this point of new departure. We exercise our responsibility by leaving him free to choose — and take the consequences. This is weaning, and we are all mothers in this. When the weaning process is arrested emotional disturbance follows and frustrated irritable children are the result. The child remains partly an infant; the adolescent partly a child. From imperfect weaning come most of the troubles that beset parents and children.

One parental attitude most essential to success in the 'weaning' of children is the joy of the parent on seeing dependence gradually give way to independence. This is that higher part of a parent's love which seeks to give rather than to possess. We must *want* to see our children moving away from us rather than clinging to us. Parents who find a sickly joy in the dependence of a son or a daughter are crippling not rearing a child. The possessive parent is the supreme egoist. The parent who loves wisely will always be urging on her fledglings to risk a little flight from the nest. We lend our children our support so that one day they will have no need for it.

C. THE HOME

My observation of Quaker homes over a long period suggests that home-making is, for most Friends, a real concern that exists as a service in its own right. In some ways it might be regarded as the foundation on which all Friends' service stands, for I am sure if Friends had neglected home life because they were so busy with their concerns outside the home this external service would have been a much poorer offering to God and man.

The good Quaker home takes its place among the more lovely evidences of Christian faith. When I recall experiences of the 'real thing' I find memory centring firmly on the morning reading and the following silent grace before the first meal of the day. This simple ceremony, the brief reading from the Scriptures or other appropriate book, quiet waiting and listening that seems to bid time and busy-ness cease so that deeper things may take hold, to me symbolize the essence of Quaker home-making. Whatever clatter may follow as cereals disappear and eggs are cracked, for this brief space tribute has been paid to the sustaining truth that the family cannot live by bread alone. This I say with conviction but with a sense of guilt and loss, for I have to confess that in our case the rush of the morning hour too often flowed over the reading, a lapse, I fear, not unknown among Friends today. But

I have no doubt that this daily reminder that God alone gives the increase of grace in the home is the best way to begin the day.

There can be no Christian home where its members are family-centred. It is strange but true that a family can be so inwardly concerned in its affections as to be essentially selfish, so closely knit and self-sufficing that it faces the world from a charmed circle into which the lives of others fail to penetrate. This is a sickly sort of family unity. The home should be the centre but not the boundary of our affections, and the quality of a family's intimate life will depend in large measure on the desire of its members to stretch outwards to join in the lives of others. There are few influences more inwardly binding than the outward concerns of parents for the welfare of people in the wider world. When parents open their home to those who need friendship, and engage their energies in socially valuable work, their children, not unobservant but not consciously observing, learn in their turn that the Christian home cannot live unto itself.

Widely as the functions of husband and wife may differ their essential equality is the basis of family life. Fatherhood and motherhood are not the same thing; there are duties best accepted by men, others uniquely associated with women. But mutual dependence implies equality of status. That is not an equal love which seeks only to dominate or to depend. But one practical obstacle to the equal sharing of activities outside family life is the inevitable separation of the mother of young children from the wide interests which easily come the way of her husband. This difficulty should be faced in the early days, for the exclusion of the mother from the interests of her husband, and later on from those of her growing children, is a situation not without danger to the later periods of motherhood. It involves a determined effort of the wife to maintain touch with her old interests or to form new ones, and deliberate planning by both parents to preserve some balance of duties in the home. Young mothers should observe that a high proportion of women who have contributed much to the welfare of mankind have had families, and sometimes large families. Family life has itself enriched their wisdom. This may be an encouragement to a young mother at a time when her best contribution to society is to rear her children. Nevertheless, if she can at the same time keep in touch either by reading or occasional contact with affairs beyond her immediate duties she will be ready for fuller engagement when her children are able to rely more on themselves. The chief need is to preserve her freshness and gradually increase her value in the home by cultivating interests outside it. Fortunately the easy way in which Friends' Meetings find a place for young parents and children helps to keep young mothers in touch with social and religious affairs well beyond the Meeting House.

All this is especially important for the woman between the ages of forty and fifty who, her family having grown up, may find herself isolated from her children and from the affairs of the world after a long period of absorption in the cares of the home. Emptiness of life is a grave danger at this age and may lead to nervous troubles and unhappiness unless she can readjust her life to new activity. But where education in girlhood has been sufficient to provide a basis for further study, and where opportunities for adult education encourage a renewal of aesthetic and intellectual interests, new sources of activity may be found. She will still be able to share ideas with her children and remain their stay even if it be by remote control. And the transition from one way of life to another will always be easier if the pressures of family life have never been allowed to crowd out the things that are eternal.

There is another question. Is it possible for women to have their careers and their babies too? That is the residual question remaining now that sex equality is taken for granted. If the freedom not to have babies means smaller families or no families at all, the loss to society will be great. But when we examine the situation at present existing we find hundreds of thousands of mothers at work and also an increasing birth rate. Our schools are bursting especially with children in the lowest age ranges. Nevertheless I have noted two danger signals. The first is an increasing number of mothers who break down under the double strain of doing a job and running a home; the second is the number of well-fed and well-clothed but maternally neglected children who appear in the juvenile court. I am inclined to think that where the mother works only to raise the material standard of living of the family this is not a sufficient reason for leaving her children too much to their own resources. Schools can never be an adequate substitute for mothers; and that is a poor view of education that sees the schools function merely as a corrective to indifferent upbringing.

There is one more question we have to face. What has Christian teaching to say about family planning? The New Testament nowhere asserts that sexual intercourse in wedlock apart from the procreation of children is wrong, although this ascetic view of marriage has crept unwarrantably into some interpretations of Christian doctrine. But does this mean that no restrictions should be placed on the number of children born in wedlock? There are several points to consider before we get a satisfactory answer to this question. In the first place, if we believe that husband and wife should share in the responsibilities of family life, the possibility of twenty-five years of unrestricted child-bearing would seem to place far too great a burden on one partner. Surely the purposes of family life are best served by producing a family of such a size that the strains of child-bearing and the rearing of children are consistent with the good health of the mother and the proper education of the children. Size is not the criterion of family quality, nor can the Christian view of the family accept the sex impulses of the husband as the primary reason for producing children. But when parents sincerely desire to build up a family in which the finest personal qualities can be cultivated in a harmonious family life, then there is very good reason to exercise care in family planning.

How should family limitation be achieved? It is here that the controversy begins. The restriction of intercourse to such rare occasions when a child is desired is not even a counsel of perfection, for it eliminates that expression of physical love which we have seen to be a creative element in the ripening of personality in both husband and wife. And on the negative side such abstention is likely to create nervous tensions that serve no good end. In my view responsible parenthood is best achieved by mutual love and respect, and by responsible use of approved means of preventing conception. But having said this it is important to add that great moral and social dangers lurk in the use of contraceptives. Even the unrestricted fertility of earlier times may be more desirable than childless or single-child marriages, where technical knowledge is abused for irresponsible sexual enjoyment or to satisfy the selfish desires of luxurious living. Such attitudes have no place in Christian marriage; they are the grand refusal of its finest joys and of its highest social purposes.

D. SIMPLICITY

In the new edition of *Christian Faith and Practice* there is an interesting section entitled 'The Art of Living' in which much is written under the heading of 'Simplicity'. This section is prefaced by a quotation from our General Advices which reads as follows:

'Carefully maintain in your own conduct and encourage in your families truthfulness and sincerity. In your style of living, in your dress and in the furniture of your houses, choose what is simple and beautiful. Encourage the reading of good books, so that the taste thus formed may instinctively reject the trivial and base.'

The interest of these simple words lies in the artless way in which the material conditioning of life is associated with life's spiritual quality. This assumption is quite basic to the Quaker view of good living. Unfortunately the popular Quaker image is the figure of the gloomy Puritan who suspects beauty, frowns on joy and rejects the fun of life. It is true of course that Quakers have not escaped those negative aspects of Puritanism that viewed with deep suspicion influences tending to divert men's minds from the serious Christian call. But Quakerism has never been deeply rooted in Puritanism, although until the later years of the last century drama, music and the other arts were not fully appreciated by Friends. All that is changed now. Even when I first encountered Friends over thirty years ago I should have described them as a merry people imbued with serious intentions. And as to the arts, I will hazard a guess that there are more Friends in proportion to their numbers in whose lives good literature, music, the drama and the visual arts and crafts count for much than there are in the general population. These influences are reflected in Quaker schools which lay strong emphasis, some educators would say too much emphasis, on the aesthetic side of education. I like to think that that lovely spirit Gerard Hoffnung, musician, caricaturist, uproarious story-teller and comic, prison visitor and Friend, represents both the light and serious sides of modern Quakerism. A man who made the prison corridors echo with healing laughter has a special place in our affections.

It is not on fun and beauty that Quakerism frowns but on luxury of life, the kind of living that Jesus had in mind when he doubted the easy passage of rich men into heaven, not because they were rich but because concentration on things turns our gaze away from the real and the eternal. We must sit light to our possessions lest they come to possess us. Used as sales-talk in our glossy magazines the phrase 'gracious living' has become a synonym for making a house an end in itself rather than a home to live in. Truly gracious living is a by-product of gracious thinking and doing, and in material things is expressed in 'what is simple and beautiful'. And true simplicity is not the rejection of beauty in our surroundings but the refusal to allow concern for things to clutter our minds to the exclusion of our Christian duties. Hence we can be comfortable without being soft, we can eat wholesome food without being gourmand or gourmet, and our luxuries should be of a kind that cater for the spirit rather than the body, reflecting neither vulgarity nor yet a snobbish preciosity, at times maybe down to earth but never trivial or mean. Tommy Handley and Shakespeare each have their place in a well-proportioned life.

The vast majority of Friends have to take care of the pennies, or shall we say the shillings, and are more likely to spend spare cash on books than upholsteries à la mode. In the more affluent homes, and of these Friends have their share, good taste is more evident than ostentation, even at the cost of many pounds. Seldom have I encountered extravagance in dress; indeed, even my male eye detects a frequency of well-worn garments among our women folk who on the whole dress for comfort and utility. For a reason I have not been able to discover large gatherings of Friends, for example Yearly Meeting, tend to encourage the open-necked shirt among males. Friends then, sit as loose in their clothes as their clothes sit on them.

Most of these unremarkable people are much concerned for affairs beyond their home, profession or business, and an examination of their shabby brief-cases or outsize utility hand-bags, as they make for their monthly and quarterly meetings, would certainly reveal papers dealing with a surprising variety of affairs concerning this world and the next. But lest it be thought that I describe a moderately affluent and educated middle-class society it must be emphasized that the majority of Friends belong to income groups where economies are necessary. Nevertheless it is sad that too few are among the less educated groups, for there is ample proof that these men and women, while lacking in academic training, bring experience of enormous value to the religious and social work of the Society. Of any single profession, teachers, whether working in Approved Schools or universities, seem to be most numerous according to our statistics. But on the whole the Society represents a fair cross-section of the middle and lower-middle groups of the national community. And I think it may be said that a central concern of Quakers is to establish Christian homes in which a gentle discipline happily consorts with reasonable freedom, and where values derived from their Quaker faith are inculcated under the conviction that children must be surrounded

'Not with the mean and vulgar works of man,
But with high objects, with enduring things.'

XVIII

CHRIST AND CAESAR

'Is it lawful to give tribute to Caesar or not?'
MARK XII, 14

'Do men gather grapes of thorns, or figs of thistles?'
MATTHEW VII, 16

AS A YOUNG soldier I served in the First World War, one of those who in the patriotic fervour of the times volunteered before my age-group was called up. I was an unthinking unit in a wild enthusiasm. There was no heroism involved, in spite of what our elders said of us; we just wanted to be in the war, in the flow that engulfed that generation. I was one of twenty-six brothers and cousins in the forces, not all of whom returned. I had never heard of pacifism or Quakers and if I had I should have thought the former a betrayal and the latter sorry patriots. I did not find myself thinking about righteous causes, only of the immediate emergency. Periods of dull acceptance, escape into the opiate of a 'good time', comradeship with the rough fellows who were my companions in arms, were all part of the show we knew as war, which in all its aspects seemed to be in parts a happy, silly, noble, stark and horrible affair demanding to be fought and won. If I had been more sensitive I should have thought more, but thinking did not begin till it was all over.

Or rather thinking began when I slowly realized that it was not all over. At the university and during the following years, that era of dying hopes, I began to see with the eyes of Wilfred Owen

> 'the truth untold,
> The pity of war, the pity war distilled.
> Now men will go content with what we spoiled,
> Or, discontent, boil bloody and be spilled.'

Was war a misdirected sacrifice? Can war turn tortured worlds to better ways? These doubts assailed me. It was such a muddle: no clear convictions except conviction of the need to have convictions.

Quakerism again came to my aid. Here seemed to be a foundation on which to stand; a simple logic, perhaps a too simple logic, but one which pointed to a new way of thinking — that war could never do what men expected it to do because it worked against the grain of the human soul. Thus by encountering the Quaker Peace Testimony I was forced to think out the Christ and Caesar problem which confronts most of us at times.

When Jesus responded to the God or Caesar challenge he did not condemn Caesar but asked us to note that the claims of God and of the State on our allegiance, although different in kind, are not necessarily opposed. Neither Jesus nor Paul suggests that the state is merely a necessary evil. They accepted the civil authority as an institution that preserved men from anarchy and made possible an ordered life. Nevertheless we are left in no doubt that man's allegiance to God transcends all other loyalties and that there may be occasions when men have to yield up one loyalty for the other. This conflict of loyalties is no simple black and white affair; almost always it comes upon us in shades of grey and in forms that challenge both reason and faith. It is usually described as a conflict between conscience and the state.

When this conflict arises we have to be certain that we do not oppose the state merely because its claims may hurt or impoverish us; our objection must be founded on more than individual caprice. Resistance to state action is fully conscientious only in so far as it contributes generally to a higher morality within the community. When, for instance, John Woolman refused to place his name to the conveyance of a human soul from one slave-master to another he was not merely stilling a disturbed conscience but striking a blow on behalf of a slave-free society. True, his conscience worried him; but he was not worried about his conscience. When conscience remains ego-centric it ceases to be 'the complete self voicing its ideals'. For conscience is not of greater account than the truth to which it has to testify. Hence conscience must operate always in that negative-positive way which is creative of good beyond the self. The corollary to 'we say No' must always be 'we say Yes'.

With this brief exposition of the nature of conscientious objection we may pass on to consider the basis of the Quaker testimony against all war. Again, as in all Quaker judgments, our peace testimony is an inevitable deduction from the doctrine of the indwelling Christ, from the conviction that the Light of Christ 'shines through all'. In our view, to take life deliberately is to cease absolutely to love our neighbour and to deny in ourselves the very quality that makes us men. Hence, the Quaker argument runs, the violence and cruelty we know as war is intrinsically evil because it violates human personality in a complete degree. But beyond this, war frustrates its own ends, even if they be good, for if there is anything quite clear about Christ's teaching it is that the means will determine the end. Figs do not grow on thistles; neither will the fruits of hatred and lust be other than destructive. In the presence of evil the Christian method is not to destroy the person who is evil but to reach to the good that is in him and build on that. As Max Plowman has said, 'pacifism is not the expression of a sentimental and exaggerated regard for the human body, but the acknowledgment of a religious reverence for the human spirit.' Hence, to Friends' way of thinking, pacifists must be ready to die but not to kill.

Is this an over-simplified statement of the issue that faces the Christian? In the sense that Jesus confronts us with a choice of methods, the one destructive and the other creative, it is not. I just cannot extricate myself from this interpretation of the Christian method of resisting evil. It seems to me to be an absolute. In opposition to this view there are those who would compare the sacrifice of the soldier in battle with the death of our Lord on the Cross, quoting a strangely irrelevant but beautiful text to prove their point: 'greater love hath no man than this, that he lay down his life for his friends.' I have no wish to disparage the courage and sacrifice of the soldier, but surely this comparison is false. Willingness to die for a principle is not the same thing as to kill for a cause. Even when inspired by the highest motives the soldier dies in an effort to destroy the enemy; but Jesus raised no hand against those who destroyed his body. The two types of sacrifice are different in kind. Against the power of evil Jesus fought to the end, not with the weapons of the soldier but alone, 'unarmed save by the Spirit's flame'.

But in the sense that it leaves us with a formidable array of unsolved problems this claim, that we are faced with an absolute, certainly is an over-simplification. It may reasonably be urged that many wars have achieved some immediate good, some security or freedom deemed of great value by its defenders. But it can never be proved that such 'good' could not have been achieved in a non-violent way, even if that way be long; whereas it can be proved that no freedom was ever gained by violence which did not leave scars that defaced the freedom won and also an aftermath fruitful of further conflict. This must always result when human action neglects the means God places at man's disposal for solving human problems. We have only to look around at the fear-tortured world we live in, after a Second World War, to accept that proposition. The means God dispenses to us are moral laws as unerring in their consequences as the physical laws of the material universe. Jesus explained the operation of these moral laws in simple phrases, like the saying about figs and thistles. We are so made, Jesus implies, that love, co-operation and unselfishness yield their appropriate fruit of harmony; and similarly, the fruits of violence, hatred and greed yield their proper harvest of destruction. In our mechanized age he might well have illustrated his theme thus: 'If you have a motor car you can put water in the petrol tank and petrol in the radiator, and you can experiment with triangular wheels; but it won't go, because it defies the laws of combustion and locomotion.'

But, the non-pacifist Christian will reply: we live in two worlds, the world of God's Kingdom and also the world of imperfect human institutions and imperfect men. We are bound by two moralities. Is it not therefore our duty to contract-in to this imperfect world which men have made, using its methods when we must and treading the higher path when we can? This is the point at which sincere men disagree. The pacifist says, if we know the laws of God we must operate them now and take the consequences; the non-pacifist says that to do so is to court destruction, to see precious liberties disappear, to connive with the strong against the weak, to yield to all the lustful forces of evil in men and nations. And, he would add, it is only because men have fought and died for the freedoms you enjoy that you pacifists can sit quietly in your homes and hold your subversive views. And, moreover, he would not be wrong. The pacifist must recognize that in this one way he is contracting out of what many good men regard as sacred duties for the preservation of the state that protects them. In war he eats food that reaches our shores at the cost of human life, and is preserved from the tribulations of invasions and oppression by men willing to fight.

There is a real dilemma here. But in fairness to the pacifist it must be said that wars are caused because the principles he preaches have been scorned and that he is perfectly willing to accept the awful consequences of his refusal to fight. Moreover, he would probably admit that when war breaks out his cause is temporarily defeated. All that remains for him to do is to stick to his principles, to relieve the suffering war inflicts at any risk to his own life, and to partake to the utmost minimum in the benefits of the state's protection. There is a searching challenge in the late William Temple's suggestion that the pacifist should indicate a willingness to contract out of the advantages as well as out of the obligations of citizenship. But in practice this is almost impossible to do.

I have tried to be fair to the critics of Christian pacifism who regard the pacifist's refusal to bear arms as a wholly negative attitude. But Friends would maintain that their attitude to war and peace is by no means negative. Being convinced that war as a means of settling disputes is entirely inconsistent with the Christian method, we believe we are performing a positively educative function in the interests of the human race and in the true Christian tradition. Our object is to preach and practise the way of reconciliation, to condemn the way of violence and to persuade men that God's way is not mad but right. We cannot accept the proposition that we must wait until love and sanity rule a world at present governed by fear before we declare the means of achieving this desired end. On the contrary we argue that fear will disappear when the causes of fear are removed. Today one of the main obstacles to rational release of international tensions is the existence of the H Bomb. The policy of more and better bombs is not likely, therefore, to increase the chances of peace. Even non-pacifists are beginning to accept this argument. But the existence of instruments for mass destruction of human life does not fundamentally affect the pacifist case against all war; it merely highlights the fantastic futility of modern war. The Christian pacifist, aware of all the arguments against him, finally asserts his belief that organized human destruction violates the spirit of man both in the destroyer and in the destroyed. When challenged to take his part in the organization of war, therefore, he is inevitably impelled to say — This I cannot do.

But today, although Christian pacifist principles remain unchanged, they have to be worked out in a far more complex and bewildering situation, for we are now faced not with massed armies and navies composed of individual combatants, but with the press-button release of forces capable of destroying a large part of the human race in minutes. And, to add to the horror, the decision to engage in genocide will be made by one or two frightened and fallible men. The criteria for such decision, moreover, are bound to be of the most elusive kind, for we are now faced not only with the possibility of a planned atomic cataclysm but with the increasing likelihood of an 'accidental war'. The tragic idiocy of this situation is thus exposed by Professor T. C. Schelling, 'one of America's foremost thinkers on the problems of nuclear strategy'. In an extracted article from the Bulletin of Atomic Scientists printed in *The Observer* (13 November 1960), Professor Schelling says:

'This whole idea of "accidental war" rests on a crucial premise — that there is an enormous advantage, in the event that war occurs, in starting it, and that each side will be not only conscious of this but conscious of the other's preoccupation with it. In any emergency when the likelihood of immediate war rises to where it is "substantial", the urge to pre-empt — to pre-empt the other's pre-emption, and to pre-empt his attempt to pre-empt our pre-emption and so *ad infinitum* — can become a dominant motive. It is hard to imagine how anybody would be precipitated into full-scale war by accident, false alarm, mischief, or momentary panic, if it were not for the urgency of getting in quick. If there is no advantage in striking an hour sooner than the enemy, and no disadvantage in striking an hour later, one can wait for better evidence of whether the war is on. But when speed is critical, the victim of an accident or false alarm is under terrible pressure to get on with the war if in fact it is a war.

So is the other country! If the Russians have an accident, we have to consider whether or not the Russians can be sure it was an accident, and whether they can be sure that we know that they know it. This is the second reason why the need for speed aggravates the problem: each side imputes to its enemy a similar urgency.'

In this situation the pacifist has a duty vastly extended beyond his former activities. The niceties of conscientious scruple have to give place to co-operation with every agency likely to rid the world of nuclear war. He will find himself working alongside those who do not share his pacifist views, but he must get his shoulder firmly alongside other shoulders pushing in the right direction.

As far as Friends are concerned this is what is happening. Quakerism is not pacifism; indeed, a few Friends are not pacifists. But Quakerism, in my view is an interpretation of Christian teaching that logically includes the pacifist witness among many other testimonies. Hence it is good to see Quaker teams permanently established at the United Nations headquarters in New York, at Geneva and at other internationally significant points throughout the world, joining forces with all agencies, religious, social and political, that seek to remove the causes of conflict and to abolish the inhuman madness of atomic war. Today no religious or conscientious scruple should prevent the Christian pacifist from engaging with non-pacifists in social and political peacemaking. But one policy regarding the abolition of atomic weapons, Friends are, I believe, on principle bound to adopt: they can be no other than unilateral disarmers.

Quite apart from this dominating issue of nuclear war there are one or two other aspects of the discussion that demand our attention. There is the question of an international police force. On this matter I am aware that I shall disappoint some of my Quaker friends, for I fear I shall depart from the absolutist position adopted by many Christian pacifists. In the first place we must make a distinction between the use of force and the use of violence. It is quite silly to say that Friends do not believe in the use of force. Physical force in restraint of the wrong-doer is entirely acceptable when used under the law by police in the performance of their duty. But the policeman's job is entirely different from the soldier's whose duty, except when he is acting as a policemen, is to defeat the enemy by destroying him. The policeman uses restrained force not to destroy the offender but to bring him to justice. The unarmed British policeman is the symbol of the police function in Britain. And, moreover, it is not on the soldiers in the local barracks on whom he relies for support, it is on the backing of the law-abiding British citizens whom he represents.

Now the soldier under international command in an international police force stands somewhere between the policeman and the ordinary soldier. He is there to keep the peace between opposing armies, to restore order and to start the civic wheel turning after civil administration has collapsed. He may have to use violence but only in the last extremity and in a minimal degree. To this extent he is a policeman. In situations of this kind, then, I concede the need for an internationally sponsored soldier police to hold the combatants apart. If we can reduce the functions of armies to this point we can abolish all the major instruments of modern war tomorrow. What an advance that would be! Thus, I compromise, and accept the charge of illogicality. But in this business of peace-making we must beware of driving an argument to its logical conclusion, for logical conclusions tend to neglect human realities.

By thus yielding to the pressure of a real and dangerous situation I am clearly departing from the tradition of Quaker pacifism. I regret this. But what worries me about the Quaker position today is the number of situations in world affairs from which Friends stand aloof but on which Friends seem able to give advice. This dilemma exercises the minds of many Friends who live nearer to the hard facts than others do. Too easily the principles that govern individual relationships are applied by Friends to immensely complicated collective situations with a naïve disregard of their complexity and too little recognition of the harrowing responsibility of men from whom a solution is demanded *now*.

This problem of the gap between principles applicable in

personal relationships and principles relevant to collective responsibility has prompted some Friends to ask such questions as these:
Has the Society anything to say about short term solutions to
existing crises? Friends are elected to Parliament but what would
a Friend do if he found himself a member or Prime Minister of
a government responsible for national defence? Why are there
Quaker mayors but no Quaker chief constables, plenty of Quaker
civil servants but no colonial governors, hundreds of social
workers but no policemen, no ambassadors but many workers
in the international field? The general answer to these questions
is that Friends have chosen occupations congenial to their outlook
on life and avoided occupations which might involve compromise
with pacifist principles. But too few Friends have honestly admitted
that there *is* a gap between their long term policy of non-violence
and the exigencies of modern civil and international affairs. To
admit this would clear the air and provide Friends with a more
realistic view of what their function in peace-making ought to
be. No interpretation of Christianity permits Christians to
remain snug in any ivory tower. The positive principle in the
working of conscience must again be emphasized —'We say No'
must always imply 'We say Yes'.

The Quaker dilemma, as far as I can see, can be resolved in
two ways. In the first place the Quaker witness against all war
must be maintained, because it is founded on Christian truth and
because this truth must be declared. The educative value of this
persistent witness has been shown in its increasingly wide acceptance among members of other branches of the Christian Church.
In all great causes there must be pioneers whose function it is to
point the way. Otherwise the world remains forever in the realm
of the second-best, governed by expedients that can never hold
back the flood of evil. On the other hand it is of the utmost
importance that Friends should recognize the nature of the
responsibilities of men who hold positions Friends themselves
would not feel free to occupy. And when policies in home or
international affairs contain elements of constructive thinking it
is the duty of the pacifist to commend and support them, straining
his conscience to the uttermost in his efforts at co-operation. A
tender conscience too often restrains us from touching pitch.
There should be more contracting-in to difficult situations and

compromising occupations so that the witness may be made in the midst of the struggle, not on the touch line. That grand Quaker stalwart McGregor Ross, who for twenty years held a high position in the Kenya Public Works Department, maintained his job and despite much opposition fought for African liberties without ceasing. He once told me of an occasion where one young assistant district officer could have prevented illegal expropriation of native land if he had had the courage to stand firm on a principle. That is what I mean by contracting-in to public services. Even a compromise in the right direction is better than leaving the field to those with whom we totally disagree. There is a wide field of service within the framework of established authority, but outside the armed and auxiliary forces, into which Friends might usefully penetrate. Nevertheless it is inevitable and right that most Friends should see their duty in healing and reconciling work and in declaring the fundamental principle that war defies the will of God.

XIX

THE CHRISTIAN AND THE SOCIAL

'Man is other men.'

BANTU PROVERB

'Jesus, like any of the Hebrew prophets, could not make a religious assertion without making a demand on social behaviour.'

JOHN MACMURRAY

A. THE TRADITION

IN THE Introduction to this book I have said that a particular appeal of Quakerism was its effortless penetration into every corner of life, into the intimately personal but also into the social and political. Throughout the history of Quakerism there has never been any doubt that to make a religious assertion is to make a demand on social behaviour. For this reason Friends can claim to be in the true tradition of the Hebrew prophets whose message was firmly founded on the conviction that God works in history. The writings of early Friends teem with references to the indivisible unity of the Christian and the social. 'O ye earthly minded men', cries Fox, 'give over oppressing the poor; exalt not yourselves above your fellow creatures; for ye are all of one mould and blood.' And Edward Burrough: 'What is there effected to this day? What true liberty to subjects more than was many years ago? What oppressions taken from the people? . . . we are for justice, and mercy and truth and peace, that these may be exalted in our nation.' How like Amos, the prophet of social righteousness, this is!

So firmly was this prophetic theme embedded in the stuff of early Quakerism that William Penn bravely applied it in an ambitious political adventure. His 'Holy Experiment' in Pennsylvania was an attempt to build, on what he thought was virgin soil, a state founded on trust, honesty and justice. But, alas, Penn was soon to learn that outside the Garden of Eden the soil on which righteous communities might be built is seldom virginal, for the human instruments at his disposal were sadly imperfect. And yet, even in its ultimate failure Penn's experiment was significant. There was enough in his initial success to prove that honest dealing yields the fruits of peace, and in his final failure to prove that self-seeking and fear produce their harvest of strife.

A less romantic figure than Penn was his contemporary John Bellers, who quite remarkably illustrated the Quaker emphasis on the relevance of personal religion to social improvement. Here was no social 'do-gooder' but a man of deep religious life. It was out of a 'true silence' that his amazing energies were projected into ceaseless social planning. He anticipated by over a century Ruskin's gospel that the only true wealth is life. He had no patience with conventional charity as a discharge of the debt owed by the wealthy to the poor, 'the labour of the poor being the mines of the rich' he declares in his plans for a College of Industry addressed to Parliament in 1695. An astonishingly modern note rings through all his proposals. He addresses Parliament on the evils of unemployment; he attempts to arouse concern for the adolescent wastage in the London streets; he anticipates by a hundred years the ideas of Elizabeth Fry and Barnardo; a century after his death Francis Place and Robert Owen find their schemes for co-operation in his earlier proposals. Our national health service is foreshadowed; he demands the reform of the criminal law six generations before it was accomplished. Bellers was the first penal reformer to test the actual effectiveness of hanging for felony, and his findings, quite distinct from his humane feelings, prompted him to oppose the death penalty, possibly the first man in history to do so.

There is no more compelling character in the annals of Quakerism than the saintly American Quaker John Woolman. In him we find the purest essence of the devotional life translated into untiring social endeavour. In a world which still divides its people into first and second class citizens on grounds of race and colour, the following words of Woolman have a poignant relevance, exactly two centuries after they were written:

'Oppression in the extreme appears terrible; but oppression in more refined appearances remains to be oppression; and where the smallest degree of it is cherished it grows stronger and more extensive. To labour for a perfect redemption from this spirit of oppression is the great business of the whole family of Christ Jesus in this world.'

Early in the nineteenth century Quaker concern for social reform gathered pace. We all know of Elizabeth Fry's work, beginning with the brutalized women prisoners of Newgate and extending into all areas of prison reform and the treatment of criminals. Her inspiration stimulated a movement for penal reform that still vigorously pursues the ends and applies the principles that emerged from her amazing devotion and insight. From this time Friends' energies were engaged in ever widening circles of social activity, not least in education. Even in the early days Friends' concern for education was made evident in numerous statements urging the Christian education of their children — a minute of 1695, for instance: 'This meeting do desire that, where Friends can, they would get such schools and schoolmasters for their children, as may bring them up in the fear of the Lord and love of his truth. . . .' Re-examining their educational resources in the early nineteenth century Friends realized that they were inadequate to deal with the new demands their awakened social consciousness laid upon them. Many schools were then founded which today are large and vigorous. As Joseph John Gurney bluntly remarked in 1831, 'We shall never thrive upon ignorance.' Adult education also became a major interest of Friends as they steadily turned their attention to the needs of the uneducated parent and worker.

A fuller realization of what their peace testimony implied in terms of positive peace-making impelled Friends into international affairs and turned their energies to service in the mission field. The visit of Joseph Sturge and two other Friends to the Tsar in 1854, in their effort to prevent the Crimean war, was the first of many reconciling missions Friends have engaged in, including missions to Palestine in 1948 and to Moscow and Peking in the 1950's. In 1870 a 'Friends War Victims Committee' was formed to render aid to the victims of the Franco-Prussian war, and its badge, the red and black star, adopted by relief workers and the Friends' Ambulance Unit in the two great world wars, became a well-known symbol of humanitarian assistance throughout and beyond the confines of Europe. From now on the Society took the world for its parish.

In 1833 came another break from the eighteenth-century quietist tradition when Joseph Pease was elected to Parliament, to be followed in a few years by John Bright. The entry of Quakers into national politics was their final admission that the good Christian had a part to play in secular affairs. But they have never been quite comfortable in the cut and thrust of politics and party strife. Service in local government has been much more congenial, and in the professions Friends are active in medicine, teaching, probation work and similar social services.

Since the First World War, then, English and American Friends have continued to respond to the changing social and international challenges of their time. The evils of unemployment, the devastations of war, the racial and colour problems, the cause of the refugee, material relief in human catastrophe, the reform of the penal system, missionary and educational service, have much occupied the thought and activities of Friends on a world-wide scale. Long experience with these problems has developed traditions and principles of action, and also considerable practical skill, in the administration of relief. These more evident activities have earned Friends a high reputation as relief workers. But the Society of Friends is not a soup-kitchen. It is a religious society. These external activities are no more than an end-result of impelling convictions that flow from the basic Quaker belief in the divine Seed in man. All Quaker social effort, and the peculiar form it takes, are derived from two principles: first, that the material conditions in which men live affect the growth of the divine principle within them; secondly, that all human effort should be founded on trust in the capacity for goodness in all men.

Hence it has seldom been the sole object of Friends' social and missionary endeavour to feed the hungry and preach the gospel. Their aim has also been to rehabilitate and educate the victims of disaster or of evil social conditions, so that the sufferers may begin again to accept responsibility for building their own lives. Roger C. Wilson, speaking from close-up experience, thus admirably describes the objectives of the relief worker:

'Most relief work begins with some obvious physical need.
But almost always there is, behind the physical need, something
much less concrete, a damaged or lonely or hopeless or hungry
spirit, and relief work which does not penetrate to this level,
directly or indirectly, consciously or unconsciously, and make
some contribution to healing is a job only partially done. . . .
Inspired relief workers cease to be external agents; like Woolman they have a sense of "being mixed in with" suffering
mankind: unselfconsciously they become part of the chaos, the
misery and the perplexity in which they move, and yet they
neither accept nor are degraded by the situation. . . . A relief
organization, then, ought to be a corporate body capable of
both common-sense and imaginative action, combined with
a natural ability to convey to others a sense of inner peace and
stability, surviving outward chaos and yet not divorced from it.'

B.   THE WELFARE STATE

Such endeavour is obviously a necessary extension of the Christian
gospel into the active relief of suffering. But difficult as its effective
performance is, great as are its demands on the intelligence and
insight of those engaged in it, the problems of relieving distress
are easier of solution than those that face the citizens of a wealthy
state who seek for greater justice and a more enlightened way of
life. Has the Christian gospel anything to say about the social,
economic and political structures of the state? Is there a Christian
ideal of social righteousness and, if so, has it any relevance to those
areas of public life in which men plan and govern? Does our
national community evoke the best qualities in its citizens?

The battle for social and economic justice that engaged the
fervour of generations just before ours has resulted in the emergence of the welfare state. Today no man need die of hunger in
Britain, although there are still many, particularly among the
aged, who have scarcely the minimum of income for sustaining a
decent life. Families who were once the recipients of charity now
sport T.V. aerials on their chimney pots. Wholesome legislation
has brought material benefit to millions who were living meagre
lives. But the citizens of Britain who 'never had it so good' still

live in an acquisitive society, in a community where people desire either riches or power or such material evidence of prosperity as keeps them up with the Jones's. Our social legislation, especially perhaps in the field of education, has opened up all kinds of new opportunity for the young, but the emphasis is all on material advancement. The vast extension of our educational provision is too much involved in our keeping up with the U.S. and U.S.S.R. in the production of instruments that will destroy us all. Thus, it is not so much in the cultivation of influences that will increase the total moral capacity of the community that the state spends our money as on the techniques that will increase our material wealth and physical ease. And the nation as a whole agrees with this expenditure, for we all like to be comfortable and to be amused and served by the gadgets our prosperity provides. We like our pleasures, and we like them strong.

In the background of our prosperity, and dominating the good offices of the welfare state, are certain characteristics of our national life that incline us to doubt whether our society is evoking the best qualities in its citizens. Before we are born our mothers are supplied with pre-natal vitamins, in our infancy we sip our state-provided orange juice, and in childhood state-provided milk. We are educated from the age of three to twenty-five (maybe) free of cost. All this is very much as it should be. I like to think that my taxes are spent in this way. But the teasing problem remains that we are in danger of producing a receiving rather than a giving generation, a getting rather than a responsible generation. The principle —'You provide the baby, we provide the rest' is not the best beginning for responsible citizenship.

There is also the problem of hugeness in our economic life, the concentration of power in vast industrial combinations. As the conveyor belt replaces the craftsman's tool the individual is removed further from the centre of decision. The Organization Man becomes the big man in our affluent society, the conformer ousts the sturdy non-conformist, and the lesser men, drafted into categories, cease to be treated as individuals. Organs of opinion, T.V. and newspapers, are concentrated in a few powerful hands and the small independent organ of protest daily faces extinction. The 'silent persuaders' subtly deployed against sales-resistance have us in thrall. Is the frequency of unofficial strikes, to the

layman seemingly for paltry reasons, a symptom of deep frustrations, beginning at 11 plus and continuing into adult life? Are
these the new forms of 'oppression in more refined appearances'
of which John Woolman warns us? If so, has the Christian
Church a message for our time in regard to it?

C. THE FUNCTION OF THE CHURCH

Few students of history would deny that the structure of any
human society affects the qualities and aspirations of the men
and women in it. Good laws and a just social organization help to
make good men, or at least prevent men from being as bad as
they might be. To say this is to say that the state, which is the
political expression of human society, has a moral purpose. As I
am writing these words in the week when tributes are pouring in
to that stalwart apostle of social justice R. H. Tawney, on his
eightieth birthday, I will allow him to say more vividly what this
really means:

'No change of system or machinery can avert those causes of
social malaise which consist in the egotism, greed, or quarrel-
someness of human nature. What it can do is to create an
environment in which those are not the qualities which are
encouraged. It cannot secure that men live up to their principles.
What it can do is to establish their social order upon principles
to which, if they please, they can live up and not live down. It
cannot control their actions. It can offer them an end on which
to fix their minds. And, as their minds are, so in the long run
and with exceptions, their practical activity will be.'

(*The Acquisitive Society*)

Tawney writes as a Christian. When he says that a political or
social system will help to determine the direction in which men
are looking —'offer them an end on which to fix their minds'—
he has the Christian end of man in mind. He reminds us, then,
that although good men will use power well, bad men will use
power ill, and that, therefore, our legislation and social organization should make bad men as powerless as possible. But it has

become more obvious, since the hopeful 1920's when Tawney wrote these words, that our present predicament is not that wicked men gain power, but that men — be they good or evil — are simply unable to control the forces they think they are commanding. Powerful interests, for example, manipulate finance under pressures that will destroy them if they are resisted. The effects on human welfare are not up for examination. Expand, absorb the lesser units or bust, seems to be the situation. The *end* of these operations is not a man or a woman but a non-personal and bigger combine-harvester, so to speak, that will more effectively produce — what? Life or dividends? William Temple once said 'We must reverse the reversal of the "natural order" which is characteristic of our civilization. The "natural order" is that consumption should control production and that production should control finance. This order has during the last half century and a half been completely inverted.' R. H. Tawney said the same thing in other words: 'property and economic activity exist to promote the ends of society, whereas hitherto society has been regarded in the world of business as existing to serve them'. Hence our vast publicity organizations, tempting never-never systems, pools and tranquillizers, all driving us away from life and living and God.

What, then, is the duty of the Christian in this complex situation where good and bad, sense and nonsense, power of wealth and poverty of spirit, whirl around in dangerous contention? What, also, is the corporate function of the community of Christians we call the Church?

When we look back to its origins we discover that the Church began as a movement and became an institution; its origin, then, was prophetic, but it was in a priestly institution that the prophetic message was embodied — and partly embalmed. For when a 'movement' becomes an institution movement tends to slow down because the preservation of the institution becomes more important than the message that gave it birth. This is as true of the Society of Friends as it is of the great historic churches. Constantly, therefore, as each generation of Christians meets a new moral and social situation they are faced with the challenge of a purpose greater than the preservation of their visible 'establishment'.

There can be no doubt what this purpose is: it is to 'preach the truth to the face of falsehood', to change human hearts and create new minds, to renew faith in Christ the incarnate Word, at the risk of extinction. 'He who would save his life shall lose it' must be the new motto for the Church's salvation from the 'establishment'. To yield up its prophetic mission is to encounter death by petrifaction. For the Church has to be the power-house that feeds its purpose through individual lives into the life of the world. The first social function of the Church, then, is to unite all its members on a common front of Christ-mindedness so that in home, school, factory and counting-house, and throughout popular culture, Christian values may percolate and circulate. Thus will its influence pass through the believers to men and women who stand on the fringe and beyond the fringe of Christian allegiance. The Christian must always be at work on those frontiers where religion impinges on the activities of the secular life.

It will be easy for most Christians to agree that this is part of the Church's function. But should the Church as an organized community step beyond that ill-defined boundary where the religious merges with the secular into the arena of political and social controversy? There are those who would limit the Church's activity to the services of consolation and spiritual renewal only, on the ground that the Church has 'no knowledge' of political and social expediencies and is not concerned with the social order. The Church must not dabble in politics, they say. Neither should it. But do not most social, political and international issues at bottom involve moral principles; and has the Church no concern with these? Was the extermination of Jewry merely an internal affair of the Third Reich? Was Suez an entirely political issue? Were those bishops wrong who declared that the denial of civic right to the African millions of South Africa is a denial of Christian brotherhood? Has the Church nothing to say to a community whose business interests seek to encourage the drinking habits of its youth, advertise pools on its public transport, devises gambling games to support religious charities,* and is at the same time responsible for the education of its young? Is the proper use of a

* I do not refer to raffles but to quite specific gambling games.

nation's wealth a matter for politicians only? If we are told that the Church, by its very nature as a divinely ordained religious institution, has no knowledge of what is good for man in his earthly passage, then we must say that this is a poor kind of Church which is so preoccupied with man's entry into the next world that it can neglect his welfare in this.

Such a proposition does not imply that bishops and presbyters should aspire to become cabinet ministers or that parsons and Quaker elders should get themselves elected to town councils. It simply means that no human activity can be removed from the province of the Christian ethic. If this be so the first social activity of the Church will be mainly concerned with the definition of ends and with the prescription of methods involved in achieving such ends. It will declare the principles out of which a noble community life can grow; it will initiate and inspire but will not elaborate details; it will declare what is needed but not how to supply the need; it will examine the impact of a nation's secular policies on the moral and physical lives of all its citizens, commending the good and condemning the destructive. The Church will usually leave to the expert the elaboration of means, while watching zealously to see that the methods employed are likely to serve the ends prescribed rather than the acquisitiveness of sectional interests. But far more important than its watch-dog function will be its educative power in producing men and women whose informed intelligence and devotion to principle measure up to the moral tasks of secular life.

There is no need to be a Quaker to accept this view of the corporate duty of Christians. One has only to examine the religious organizations of this and other nations to realize how generally Christians now extend religious activity into the social sphere. And it is remarkable that it is in this sector of religious endeavour that denominational barriers have most easily and profitably broken down.

We turn now to a more particular problem that today greatly exercises the minds of Friends in their attempts to apply Quaker principles to the work of the world. In the old days of the small family business it was difficult but not impossible for Quaker employers to apply Christian principles in their relations with employees, and Friends have established good traditions in this area of industrial life. But today, in the era of hugeness, it is far more difficult. The day of paternalism is past. Nevertheless, we are still faced with the Christian challenge in industrial relations and government. The issue may be simplified in the form of a question: Is it possible for committees to love one another? The problem is posed in this way because the management of vast undertakings no longer permits the close personal relationships possible in the past. Hence we ask, for example: Can a board of directors love the T.U.C.; can the British Transport Commission love the Transport and General Workers' Union?

The answer must be in the negative, for love can operate only between persons. We can love our friends and our enemies whom we have seen; in a more remote way we can love a Bantu or an Eskimo whom we have not seen; but we cannot love the United Nations. And yet, if we assume, as we should, that industrial magnates and trade unionists and Members of Parliament are, as individuals, capable of loving persons, and that the object of their activities is not to get rich by any means but to serve the highest human ends by the best means, then there emerges the remote possibility of a reconciling situation. Love may be sadly diluted as it trickles through the filter of the negotiating or election machinery, but if a sincere concern for human welfare, rather than for sectional interests, dominates the deliberations then, to some degree, love may be said to operate. The impersonality of corporations and committees can only be made personal by the convictions of those who operate them. If we cannot expect committees to love one another is it too much to expect them to base their decisions always on the assumption that people matter more than property; that at the end of the chain of consequences there is always a man or a woman, a boy or a girl? To care for people, no matter how big or complex an organization he may work in, is the duty of the Christian. But how much harder it is for him to make his principles effective than it is for the teacher, doctor or social worker who work always on the personal level and who actually get their wages for doing what the man in industry may have to fight for.

And so, while we bear the new burdens of prosperity, as morally enervating as the old evils of poverty, we are still faced with the fact that our wealthy communities do not evoke the best qualities in their citizens. There is still laid upon the Christian the duty of changing social structures and industrial organizations that appeal to our baser desires and inhibit men's capacity to respond to their higher promptings. We have still to learn that gadgets do not release men from poverty of spirit, from mean ambitions and from the evils of social strife. The world seems to be divided into three groups of men: those who believe man is incorrigibly evil; those who think that, given the chance, he will respond to good; and those who, in the terms of the Gallup Poll, 'don't know'. The last group constitute a suitable field for the Christian to plough.

One of the means by which we might escape from our dilemma is to resolve our inner conflict by turning away from our own prosperity to the poverty of the undeveloped peoples. The obverse of our shield of wealth is their need. And our wealth is not only in sterling and dollars, but in the vast pool of educated and technically equipped manpower that serves us too much and them too little. In the continent of Africa, for instance, there are needs in education, health, social and economic development that call for our response. But beyond these there is a call to respect the emerging claims of human dignity made by subject peoples who now struggle towards a precarious independence. Can we learn to give without expecting gratitude; can we serve where once we ruled, can we get 'mixed in' with Africans, 'surviving outward chaos and yet not divorced from it'?

In any services Friends may offer in Africa or Asia, or anywhere else, it is important that they should not become sentimental about those for whom they work. George Orwell once remarked that if he thought the poor were more virtuous than the rest of us he would always vote Tory to keep them poor. The truth about the African or Asian is that he is no less frail when challenged with the deceitfulness of riches than we are, and no more likely to make good use of increasing wealth and power than his already wealthy neighbours in the West. The African politician, official, or employer will not be found to be more faithful to the general interest or more generous to his employee than his counterpart in Europe or America. The reign of law will be no more, and probably, less respected in the new independent countries than in the old regimes; probity in business and government no more evident and the scramble for power no less acute. In the ecstasy of independence men are easily led to believe that a new heaven and a new earth are easily achieved; hence the cure of poverty no less than respect for law may go by default among peoples who have attributed their woes only to their own subjection to an alien race. Part, then, of our service to the emerging independent states is to help them to avoid our mistakes and to found their communities on principles higher than those operating in political patronage and the market place. This is the arena in which the Christian must face the lions of a deceitful prosperity.

The Christian and the social are one. The world in which we live cannot emerge from its suffering save by the devotion of men and women whose minds know something of Christ's Kingdom and use its standards as a measure of human advancement. They will fail if they are content to be members of a church or other religious society which has no aim beyond the preservation of its own existence. The pierced hands of our re-crucified Lord are in our midst, beseeching us to empty ourselves of the cluttering fears that bid us linger in our old content, to fill ourselves with God's unhasting, unchanging purpose, taking into the sad world of divided men the undivided Mind of Christ.

XX

EPILOGUE

AN ORDINARY PEOPLE

ARE THESE beliefs and practices I have described peculiar; peculiar in the sense of 'odd', outlandish, even ridiculous? Are they of a kind that separates Quakers from the general community of ordinary men and women, forcing them to live apart in a closed circle of eccentric custom? I ask this question in these concluding words because Quakers have for so long been regarded as a 'peculiar people'. A century and a half ago there may have been reasons for setting them apart as queer folk who wore distinctive garments, worshipped in silence, refused to pay tithes, addressed each other in archaic terms (and some still use the rather attractive 'thee' and 'thou'), refused to go to war or to swear oaths, and were known for honest dealing. Some of these peculiarities have now gone and some are no longer regarded as peculiar.

There was a day when Quakers were tolerated as harmless nuisances, awkward non-conformists living on the fringe of a tolerant community. Today the Society of Friends is regarded by many people as a useful relief organization and for that reason to be encouraged; and by some as a mildly subversive pacifist group whose usefulness just compensates for its irritating views. Friends tend to be praised for their outward activities which they regard as secondary, and neglected for their particular witness to the Christian faith which they regard as central and vital, the source of every concern that projects them into the world's suffering.

Friends are most concerned that their view of God's relationship to men — their faith that God's love works through men reconciling them to one another, their conviction that to answer that of God in other men is the Christian means to moral progress and peace — should be accepted more widely than it is. But I have a fear that Quakerism cuts least ice when Quakers receive the world's approval. People speak well of us today, more than ever before. So, we have been warned. And yet, in spite of this approval, our numbers have remained almost stationary in the British Isles for half a century, new convincements just keeping pace with loss of members through death and resignation. There is something queer here. Clearly those who commend us have no wish to join forces with us. Is this because we are still regarded as a peculiar people, sometimes nice to know but awkward to live with? If so, I am puzzled by this judgment, for since I have been a member of the Society I have lived very much outside it, in the sense that my work has taken me into spheres where religious profession had no consequence, and I have not noted that my Quakerism was an obstacle to close friendships among non-Friends. With this personal experience to guide me I have a suspicion that it is those who do not know Friends well who have views about our peculiarity and exclusiveness.

I think this disturbing situation is more likely due to a mistaken view of the virtues of Friends than to a true view of their failings; and also to a false view of the beliefs of Friends rather than to a true idea of the amazing latitude permitted in the wide span of the Quaker expression of Christianity. Friends are a mixed group of people who take life earnestly but not solemnly. They are not puritans, although they accept mild religious and social disciplines, not for the cramping of life but rather for the enrichment of living by a full enjoyment of God's creation and of the product of man's genius in art and science in all its most vivid expression. They are not scriptural fundamentalists but modern Christians who accept the findings of biblical scholarship, and are convinced of the relevance of the Christian gospel to personal living and social progress. For the firm believer, equally with the honest doubter, Quakerism is a wonderfully congenial home, for we ask no more of either than that he should be a seeker. Remembering my own experience, I am particularly concerned with those of a religious turn of mind for whom nevertheless, an authoritarian church or naïve enthusiasm or biblical literalism are alike offences to reason and obstacles to spiritual independence. This paragraph, then, is an invitation from one who was once in the wilderness to those who are still perplexed, to risk a journey in the company of fellow seekers who believe that faith comes by working and observing, and also by experimenting with the little faith we have.

At this point I turn from Quakerism to ultimate and bigger things.

There are, it seems to me, three ways of dealing with life, all of them noble in their way, but not equally fruitful. I am going to present the first two of these views in the words of very able men whose opinions we are bound to treat with respect. The first describes the position of the modern humanist and is quoted from Walter Lippmann's *A Preface to Morals:*

'And so the mature man would take the world as it comes, and within himself remain quite unperturbed. When he acted, he would know that he was only testing an hypothesis, and if he failed, he would know that he had made a mistake. He would be quite prepared for the discovery that he might make mistakes, for his intelligence would be disentangled from his hopes. The failure of his experiment could not, therefore, involve the failure of his life. For the aspect of life which implicated his soul would be his understanding of life, and, to the understanding, defeat is no less interesting than victory. It would be no effort, therefore, for him to be tolerant, and no annoyance to be skeptical. He would face pain with fortitude, for he would have put it away from the inner chambers of his soul. Fear would not haunt him, for he would be without compulsion to seize anything and without anxiety as to its fate. He would be strong, not with the strength of hard resolves, but because he was free of that tension which vain expectations beget. Would his life be uninteresting because he was disinterested? He would have the whole universe, rather than the prison of his own hopes and fears, for his habitation, and in imagination all possible forms of being. How could that be dull unless he brought the dullness with him? He might dwell with all beauty and all knowledge, and they are inexhaustible. Would he, then, dream idle dreams? Only if he chose to. For he might go quite simply about the business of the world, a good deal more effectively perhaps than the worldling, in that he did not place an absolute value upon it, and deceive himself. Would he be hopeful? Not if to be hopeful was to expect the

world to submit rather soon to his vanity. Would he be hopeless?
Hope is an expectation of favours to come, and he would take
his delights here and now. Since nothing gnawed at his vitals,
neither doubt nor ambition, nor frustration, nor fear, he would
move easily through life. And so whether he saw the thing as
comedy, or high tragedy, or plain farce, he would affirm that
it is what it is, and that the wise man can enjoy it.'

Here is the neo-Stoic speaking in the true tradition of that
ancient Stoicism which was a retreat for honest men in a
decadent society. Does it satisfy you?

The next world-view comes from William James's *Varieties of
Religious Experience* in the well-known paragraph on his faith in
the 'over belief'.

'What the more characteristically divine facts are, apart from
the actual inflow of energy in the faith-state and the prayer-
state, I know not. But the over-belief on which I am ready to
make my personal venture is that they exist. The whole drift
of my education goes to persuade me that the world of our
present consciousness is only one out of many worlds of
consciousness that exist, and that those other worlds must
contain experiences which have a meaning for our life also;
and that although in the main their experiences and those of
this world keep discrete, yet the two become continuous at
certain points, and higher energies filter in. By being faithful in
my poor measure to this over-belief, I seem to myself to keep
more sane and true. I can, of course, put myself into the sectarian
scientist's attitude, and imagine vividly that the world of
sensations and of scientific laws and objects may be all. But
whenever I do this, I hear that inward monitor whispering the
word 'bosh'! Humbug is humbug, even though it bear the
scientific name, and the total expression of human experience,
as I view it objectively, invincibly urges me beyond the narrow
'scientific' bounds. Assuredly, the real world is of a different
temperament — more intricately built than physcial science
allows. So my objective and my subjective conscience both
hold me to the over-belief which I express. Who knows
whether the faithfulness of individuals here below to their own

poor over-beliefs may not actually help God in turn to be more effectively faithful to his own greater tasks?'

This takes us a little further. It is at least a positive affirmation of belief. But does it not lack a clarity of outline, a definition of direction and a cutting edge? It is a declaration of a way of looking at things, truly of immense importance, but it does not tell us where to go and how to get there. It does not affirm enough. The faith we need is bound up with the conviction that behind the world is a God who can and will transform it. Belief in God as a physicist or mathematician *makes no difference*. Belief in a Creator God has little reference to our share in his creation. Christian faith is founded on our belief in a Redeemer-God who will help us to remake ourselves and whom we can help to make all things new. Such a belief is more than an 'over-belief' and is much more likely to 'help God in turn to be more effectively faithful to his own greater tasks'. And if it does not affirm the *certainty* of ultimate good (for that depends partly on us) it at least points to the possibility of ultimate good or of our chances of progressing towards it. For belief in a Redeemer-God enables us to see dimly through the murk an *order of goodness* working to a good end. To belong to this order makes co-operation with God a habit of life and the fulfilment of His will for us a greater hope, on the condition that we remain faithful and true.

Such a faith, uncomplicated as it is, nevertheless demands a leap of the imagination beyond the restraining grip of reason. But if truly held in all its simplicity, it transforms the ordinary experiences of life into a knowledge controlled by sane and healing ideals; it satisfies the needs of human kind equally in their solitude and in the press of the social struggle; it provides a sense of direction just at those points of crisis when purity of purpose is most demanded; it enables us to place our faltering hand in the supporting hand of the Most High, who will lead us on to victory against the mighty forces that might otherwise overwhelm us. This faith is power; and the symbol of this power is the figure of a Man, hanging helpless on a cross for the sake of a principle. The lesson this abandoned Figure teaches us is that men have now to exert themselves only against the circumstances that bind them, and no longer against their fellow men.

BOOKS

There exists an extensive literature on Quakerism. Here is a very short list of books useful for an introduction to the subject.

George Fox's Journal, edited by John Nickalls — Cambridge University Press.

Journal of John Woolman — Dent (Everyman).

Christian Faith and Practice in the experience of the Society of Friends. (Friends House, Euston Road, London, N.W.1.)

Brayshaw, A. Neave: *The Quakers, Their Story and Message* — Allen and Unwin.

Brinton, Howard: *Friends for 300 Years* — Harper (New York).

Fry, A. Ruth: *John Bellers: Quaker, Economist and Social Reformer* — Cassell.

Jones, Rufus M.: *The Faith and Practice of the Quakers* — Methuen.

Loukes, Harold: *The Discovery of Quakerism* — Harrap.
       Friends and Their Children — Harrap.
       Friends Face Reality — Bannisdale Press.

Vipont, Elfrida: *The Story of Quakerism* — Bannisdale Press.

Whitney, Janet: *John Woolman, Quaker* — Harrap.

Wilson, Roger C.: *Quaker Relief* — Allen and Unwin.

The Swarthmore Lectures (Allen and Unwin) published annually deal with various aspects of Quakerism.